C000180184

Praise for
IT'S GOOD TO SAY THA

"In a series of thoughtful letters, Michael thanks the people who have touched his life: not just the positive role models, but the negative ones too; not just the favored family members, but also the dysfunctional ones; not just the people he appreciated, but also the others—you know the ones! With an eye for detail and a deep understanding of human nature, he invites us into his world, and offers us an insightful and refreshing way to look back and be grateful for our own."

—DONNA BEARDEN
Author of *Finding More Me: Journaling to Go Soul Deep* and *Mandala Messages: Do Not Fear Your Potential*, Photo-Mandala Artist

"The delicate details that grace each letter show the profound lessons and gifts that can exist in our relationships. Michael's gratitude for each of his connections shines a warm light upon respect, understanding, healing, and unconditional love."

—JULIANNE HAYCOX
Author of *Conversations with Grace*

"A heartwarming and heartfelt tribute to loved ones and experiences across a lifespan. Woven throughout these love letters are fascinating antidotes of a life well lived, each containing an individual message of insight and gratitude. Collectively, a fascinating and lovely read!"

—MARCI WOLFF OBER, LMFT
Author of *The KrazyGirl (&Guy) Parent Survival Guide*

It's Good to Say Thank You

By Michael Coccari

© Copyright 2022 Michael Coccari

ISBN 978-1-64663-634-1

All rights reserved. No part of this publication may be reproduced, stored in a retrieval system, or transmitted in any form or by any means—electronic, mechanical, photocopy, recording, or any other—except for brief quotations in printed reviews, without the prior written permission of the author.

Published by

 köehlerbooks™

3705 Shore Drive
Virginia Beach, VA 23455
800–435–4811
www.koehlerbooks.com

IT'S
GOOD
TO
SAY
THANK
YOU

MICHAEL COCCARI

VIRGINIA BEACH
CAPE CHARLES

TABLE OF CONTENTS

INTRODUCTION:
Letters of Remembrance and Gratitude

AT THE AGE OF SIXTY-FIVE, I felt compelled to look back at some of the people who have had the most significant and lasting impact on me and to express my remembrance and gratitude. I suppose it is natural at my stage of life to make some calculations about the nature of relationships and how they have helped shape my identity, enriched my experiences, and made possible my accomplishments. It feels good to say "Thank you."

As I began to make a concerted effort to remember details and nuances surrounding people and events, a letter format seemed to be the best way to organize my memories. Unifying the structure of these letters is a strong desire to express my gratitude for the catalytic roles people have played in my life. Regardless of the disappointments and failures I carry with me, to have been so deeply and lastingly touched by so many remarkable and wonderful people remains a true, deep, and abiding blessing.

This process has served as a powerful reminder of how affirming and invigorating it is to say, "Thank you."

To the people in these pages who are deceased, I hope that I was able to convey my thanks to them while they were alive. If that is not the case, I hope that in some mystical way these letters of thanks are in another realm being felt.

To the people in these pages who are still living, I hope that my letters will not be the last ways I find to offer my humble, heartfelt "Thanks."

PART ONE: YOUTH

DEAR HOMETOWN BAR OWNER,

There aren't too many circumstances in which young children hanging out in a bar would be deemed appropriate. There are no circumstances in today's world in which a school bus stop would be established directly in front of a bar. But in the early 1960s in the small city of Monessen, Pennsylvania, circumstances were vastly different.

My school bus stop was located on the corner where a neighborhood bar, then referred to as a beer garden, was situated. In winter, when the temperatures were in single digits or the teens, and when snow or sleet was falling, the bar opened its doors to a small group of elementary aged kids as we waited for the bus to pick us up. The owner opened his doors at 6 AM for hardcore drinkers and he served a limited menu as well. He had a stove just inside his front door and he positioned us around it so we could keep warm and dry. His customers welcomed us and cleaned up their language out of respect for our virgin ears.

In those days, school was rarely delayed or canceled. Buses ran, schools opened, students gathered at bus stops, and inclement weather was accepted as a fact of life. We pulled on our coats, gloves, scarves, earmuffs, hats, and galoshes and made our way to school.

I can see clearly broad-shouldered men sitting around a horseshoe-shaped bar with bottles of Iron City and Rolling Rock beers on the counter, shot glasses filled with Crown Royal, and an occasional plate of bar food. The atmosphere was warm and steamy, the conversation loud but respectful, and the owner happy to offer refuge for shivering children.

Over the years, I logged quite a few hours in the bar, so many that I felt like a "regular." On Fridays, when my parents would send me there to pick up fish sandwiches, a tradition in many neighborhood households, I had familiar faces to greet and converse with.

I am thankful for all the hospitality extended to me when it wasn't owed or expected. I also can't help feeling nostalgic for an era when children could walk to a bus stop without the accompaniment of adults, could hang out in a bar without exposure to inappropriate language or behavior, and without fear of violence breaking out. The sense of communal care burned as warm as the bar's stove.

DEAR SISTERS OF ST. JOSEPH,

For many people, mere mention of the Catholic Church conjures images of priests who lead shadow lives as sexual predators. Given what we've learned about the church over the last few decades, this perception is understandable, but it's far from the whole story. I'd like to present another side and give thanks to the nuns and priests that I encountered as a child in school and church settings.

My parents decided to enroll me in parochial school beginning in first grade. I loved my public kindergarten class, but that teacher recommended St. Cajetan's School, and my parents agreed. I had no choice in the matter. This decision meant that nuns would be my teachers, with priests and a monsignor delivering special instruction weekly. I had no preconceived notions. I had awareness of the school's existence, as it was located next door to my church, so I was used to seeing it every Sunday.

In 1960, the potential influence of the Vatican on a US government policy emerged as a campaign issue for the nation as John F. Kennedy and Richard Nixon vied for the Presidency, but church sex scandals had yet to arise widely in public awareness.

Sister Marie Dominic was my first-grade teacher, and I could not fathom a better introduction to Catholic school. I remember her being quite young, although the nun's habit obscured all but her eyes, nose, mouth, forehead, and small portions of cheeks and chin. She was the most gentle, kind-hearted, compassionate teacher imaginable. Despite her floor-length nun's habit, she moved like an athlete, graceful, fluid, and assured. Her eyes glistened like stars and seemed to envelop one in an aura of comfort and ease. I felt nurtured and protected, as any first grader should feel.

At first, the habit she wore was distracting and intimidating. The tight-fitting coif, a kind of cap, seemed to cut into her forehead, cheeks, and chin. The guimpe, stiff and white, covered her shoulders and chest. The headdress and shoe-length, starkly black tunic seemed all of a piece, and large rosary beads dangled at her side. But Sister Marie Dominic wore her nun's habit so naturally that within a short period I stopped focusing on it and simply accepted it as she obviously had. She allowed us to ask questions about her nun's habit and it all but disappeared when she stood by my desk to offer encouragement and praise.

Despite all this regalia, Sister Marie Dominic was my first crush, which later seemed sacrilegious given her status as a nun. But what does the heart of a first grader know of moral complexity?

Sister Boniface was my second-grade teacher. She was on the opposite spectrum of age, but just as gentle, kind-hearted, and compassionate as Sister Marie Dominic. She seemed like an ever-present grandmother, matronly, formal, and nurturing. Both nuns created safe, wholesome learning environments, enabling me to build a strong academic foundation, which complimented my father's teaching quite well.

I particularly remember the careful attention the nuns displayed in making sure we all took proper care of our winter coats, gloves, coats, and galoshes. Without their organization system and attention to detail, we would have all lost our winter belongings in a matter of days.

I also remember how the nuns taught us to behave in church, blessing ourselves with holy water, genuflecting properly, keeping our hands folded symmetrically in prayer, kneeling in the pews without slouching, and following the cues of the priests and monsignor.

The nuns were masters at sharpening our sustained concentration powers by getting us to memorize prayers, Bible verses, details from Bible stories, and names and dates. I attributed my ability years later in high school to memorize Latin verbs and their declinations, as well as all the bones and muscles in the body, to the hard work of the nuns in my primary grades.

In third grade, I had a lay teacher who turned out to be an aunt through marriage, and who wisely and much to my relief separated her family ties to me from her duties as a teacher. In her classroom, I was just another student, undeserving of special dispensations. Looking back at my third-grade report card (my father kept a file for every year of my school, complete with report cards, photos, work samples, and miscellaneous documentation of events and trips), I earned Bs and Cs, evidence that I received no special allowances.

In fourth grade, Sister Michael tested me in many ways. Having a namesake for a teacher was far from an advantage, and a source of much teasing from classmates. Sister Michael was a taskmaster and had no tolerance for laziness, lack of effort, or mischief. But she, like Sister Marie Dominic and Sister Boniface, was an exemplary teacher. These three nuns, as well as my aunt and another lay teacher in fifth grade, inculcated in me a foundation of knowledge, skill, and an appetite for learning that fueled my academic success through graduate school. I am deeply indebted to them all.

The priests and monsignor who interacted with students in the classroom—and of course in church—were models of wisdom and integrity. They too helped create a code of attitude, philosophy, and conduct that prepared me exceedingly well for matriculation in public school. Their solemnity was always leavened with kindness.

Never was there ever the slightest hint of inappropriate behavior from the nuns or clergy. They provided me with a powerful introduction not merely to religious doctrine but more importantly to religious thought. Their teaching was humane, nurturing, and empowering. They treated us like we were young theologians by posing complex questions, helping us formulate rudimentary responses, and giving us examples of their answers.

In later decades, as church scandals emerged, I have thought often of my experiences in the care of the Catholic Church. The church emissaries who cared for me were truly holistic in their teaching, attentive and dedicated to students' personal, academic, emotional, behavioral, and spiritual dimensions. I'm grateful for their lessons and examples that I'm still prodigiously benefitting from.

DEAR MOTHER,

You have been gone for six years. I can't blame you for leaving when you did, as you were here for nearly ninety-four years. Who could disagree with your decision that you had lived long enough? But I still miss you terribly. I cannot fill the emptiness in my heart created by your death. I'm not sure I want to fill it. It is a fitting tribute that it remains a space forever unfilled.

The memories I carry do not fill the space. They accentuate it, deepen it, intensify it. If that were not the case, my life would be diminished. I am grateful that my memories are still so vibrant, possessing their own instinct for survival, and coming to me of their own accord. I hold them as one holds an infant, not wanting to surrender it to time's own uses.

Lately I've been reliving a scene from my childhood. The year was 1964. I was nine; you were forty-four. While you prepared dinner in the kitchen, I stood tethered to our mid-century modern stereo console, listening over and over to Simon and Garfunkel's *The Sound of Silence*. Although I could not fully comprehend the meaning of the lyrics, the voices, so delicate and evocative, enchanted and mesmerized me. I was at an age when music infused one's body with overpowering energy and meaning—when one used music to escape earthly coils and seemingly exist in a different realm.

I shyly, softly, sang along, and even tried out a few unsure dance moves, careful not to let you catch me in the act, self-conscious and frightened to reveal such raw feeling.

Half a century later, I can still allow my mind to be overtaken by your measured movements. I can still be stunned by the way you labored in that small and inadequate kitchen with such optimism, love, and devotion. I can hear the heels of your flats tapping on the cheaply tiled floor. You were a dancer performing a choreography that only you could fully apprehend. I can see the stovetop and counter crowded with pots and pans, your personal arrangement of order and refuge. I can see you with hunched shoulders darting in and out of my sightline as you leave the stove and sink to set the table. We were bound by a similar desire to occupy and explore our own private worlds.

Then, I was only beginning to understand your solitary life, which you carved out in the small space that my father's anger, frustration, and disappointment didn't fill. I wonder if you too were secretly listening to the stereo with more than my superficial understanding of what Simon and Garfunkel were singing about. I will hold this question until I am hopefully able to ask you directly.

I am so thankful that you allowed me a private space in which to play music of my choice, begin to feel emotions inspired by the music, and express what I was feeling through physical movement. I am also eternally thankful that you shielded me from your loneliness until I was emotionally able to comprehend and empathize with it.

DEAR FATHER,

As a child I watched you routinely rise early to dig your car out of snow and ice in order to go to work. We lived in a small town thirty miles outside of Pittsburgh and you worked in the big city. We lived in a home that didn't have a garage and you refused to allow harsh winter weather to prevent you from going to work.

Why I was awake at three or four in the morning to witness your stubborn dedication has been lost to my memory. But the sight of you bundling up and shoveling your tires clear of snow is forever seared into my consciousness. Often you had to carve a path just to reach the car. I can clearly see the exhaust smoke funneling upwards in our yard. I can see your back bending into the drifts of snow and your shoulders heaving in solitary desperation to find your tires and excavate a path for an exit.

Any rational person would have simply decided to stay home, to not fight so hard against unforgiving conditions, to not risk such a treacherous drive without benefit of four-wheel drive or chains. But your definition of rationality was modified by irrational persistence. And your sense of duty stubbornly stood up to concession, then and throughout your life.

Sometimes I stood at the door, begging you to let me help. I think a few times you relented and for a little while I pushed a shovel around ceremoniously and precociously, thinking I was actually aiding your effort, mostly getting in your way. When I couldn't keep from shivering and before my lips turned blue, you sent me back into the house to thaw out.

At the time I had no understanding of how you relished the challenge winter provided you, how you were gratified to exert your will over natural forces, how you felt proud to be at your desk when others chose the saner decision to stay home and wait for favorable conditions. For you it was a game, an adventure, a challenge. Only later did I understand that you were driven to behave as you did, defying reason, giving yourself a test that only you could assess and truly value.

My lifelong fondness for and habit of rising early, I trace back to the example you set on those winter mornings some sixty years ago. You were doing so much more than digging your car out of snow and ice. You were teaching me lessons about hard work, stubbornness, will, solitary office, raw insistence. Those lessons have served me well and kept me close to you always.

For a time, I was blessed to live in a mountainous region. There were many days when I had to scrape ice off my vehicle windows, shovel a path off the driveway, and set off to work when the wiser decision would have clearly been to stay home. Unlike you, I had the advantage of a four-wheel drive truck with winter tires and plenty of road clearance, chains always at the ready. I relish those days, feeling close to you, reliving my childhood memories, seeing you anew in our backyard, exerting your determination to prevail over inclement weather, meeting the fierce force of nature with your own internal fierce force of will.

Thank you for the example you set, and for willing me a lifelong preference to use early mornings to call forth my own sense of fortitude and exertion, and for giving me a prescription to reinvigorate my sense of being alive and connected to nature.

DEAR JUDY,

To fully appreciate you, my sister, I feel a need to go back to the year 1966. That year still beats in my chest with the intensity and insistence of the heart in Poe's iconic short story, "The Tell-Tale Heart." To say that that year was momentous would be a supreme understatement. It reverberates in my consciousness with hurricane force. We have talked about it occasionally, but never to the depth I feel a need to remember it now.

Our father made a unilateral decision to move from Pennsylvania to California, to follow you and your husband, who had decided to trade an east coast teaching job for a west coast one, thereby doubling his salary. Our father had also decided to commit to a second tour of duty in Vietnam, and then to retire from his twenty-five-year Army career.

As this was a tumultuous move from one side of the country to the other, and from small-town life to suburban sprawl, and from

the insulation of extended family to the exile of strangers, our father
decided that you and your husband and our mother and I would all
live together in a rental house at least for the year-long duration of
his service in Vietnam. Upon his return from Vietnam, we would buy
houses to make our move to California permanent.

Years later, our father liked to say that in 1966 he courageously
broke familial bonds and moved his immediate family to California.
But the truth is that you and your husband had decided to move
first, and our father not only joined your exodus but took credit for
the idea. Maybe he did so because you and your husband were living
with our parents when the two of you made your decision. Maybe
he was trying to shield you both from the harsh criticism of family
members who could not understand our exit. Maybe his ego was
too big and fragile for him to admit that the move wasn't his idea.
You always allowed him to display and enjoy that patriarchal pride.
I admire you for that, though I have never told you so directly.

We have never talked about the goodbyes we each had to say.
Mine were traumatic; I suspect yours were more so given the eleven-
year age gap between us. You were in your early twenties, newly
married, and having to say goodbye to friends that you grew up
with, your bridesmaids, and co-workers from your accounting job.
I was a fifth grader with only a handful of friends and schoolmates
to leave. Still, the gravity of my goodbyes surpassed anything I had
ever experienced at that time. I felt as if all I had ever known was
suddenly being swept away by a monstrous wave, and I was floating
into some dark oblivion without the ability to touch or even see the
ground. Perhaps for you it wasn't as bad. You were, after all, setting
out on a new adventure with your husband. You were carving out a
fresh life, fulfilling personal needs that transcended geography and
history. I was simply being relocated, like cargo.

Being torn away from family all these years later remains a
wound that will never heal. I can still feel my body squeezed to the
point of physical pain by an uncle who wept at our departure beyond

reasonableness. His uncontrollable weeping spurred my weeping to a catastrophic level. Our father reprimanded me at our car door after he pulled me away from his brother. He told me that I had to act like a man as we drove up the small hill and away from all I had ever known. To this day, I can feel my uncle's body trembling and heaving inconsolably. Our father looked mysteriously joyful as he slid behind the wheel and pointed the car toward California.

Somewhere in the middle of the country, as I lay in the back seat, looking at the sky, I began to think I was entering a world created in my imagination by the music of the Beach Boys. What else did I know of California? Nothing. All I had to attach my imagination to were mental images inspired by Beach Boys' songs. By the time we reached California, I had tempered my sadness with innocent but vibrant fantasies about heading toward a "Surfin' Safari," playing on the beach with "Little Surfer Girl[s]," and "Help[ing] Rhonda" and "Get[ting] Around" with "The Little Old Lady From Pasadena."

I know from conversations with you through the years that you had dreamy expectations about Beverly Hills mansions and Rodeo Drive shopping sprees. How naïve we both were.

We moved into a cracker box house in a worn out neighborhood on Nixon Street in the city of Lakewood. Where that was in relation to the beach and Beverly Hills, we had no clue. The house, painted a scatological brown with sickly yellow trim, endlessly depressed us. When the cross-country moving truck pulled up, it seemed to dwarf the house.

Seeing all our worldly possessions in the garage, stacked floor to ceiling, made us cry. Trying to figure out how we would fit in the cramped rooms made us want to return to Pennsylvania.

Our father had no time to indulge our miseries. He was getting ready to depart to Vietnam, where the war was raging. Our petty grievances were not worth his attention.

Our mother set about acclimating to a new kitchen, which in my mind looked like something out of a *Roy Rogers* TV episode.

It was decorated in bright yellow with intricately carved wooden shelves, with a farmhouse picnic table claiming all the open space. She adjusted to the move by concentrating on setting up the kitchen, locating pots and pans and assorted cooking utensils in the cardboard boxes that were randomly stacked in the garage. Your husband readied himself for a new school and new students. You and I mostly sat in the small living room, our senses numbed by dramatic change, feeling lost and disoriented.

The bedroom you and your husband would occupy was tiny. You and Roger would have to shuffle and scrape against the walls as you maneuvered around your double bed. The closet was too small for even your clothes, much less Roger's. It was decided that he would keep his clothes in my bedroom closet, which was barely large enough for mine, much less his. My clothes would be kept in a small dresser. I can still see Roger entering my bedroom in early morning darkness, standing in front of my closet, and pulling out his clothes for that day of teaching.

The irony of the closet situation caused much pain. Our father had built you and Roger an enormous closet on one entire wall of the extra-large bedroom that you two occupied in our old home after getting married. It was one of his wedding presents to you and an extravagance that made adjusting to our new conditions especially difficult.

In hindsight, concerns about closets seem so self-indulgent and petty. At the time, though, it brought into doubt the wisdom of the move.

With our father 8,000 miles away in Vietnam, your husband preoccupied with a new teaching position at a Long Beach junior high school, and our mother immersed in setting up a new household in a foreign place, you and I were often together, an isolated dyad trying to come to terms with such a huge change in geography and lifestyle. You helped me—more than anyone—adjust to a radically different school experience, going from a small parochial school to a gigantic public school, where I was enrolled in one of six sixth grade classrooms. You helped me comprehend the postures and behaviors and conversations of the parade of high school students who passed by our house twice a day. Together, we listened to James Brown and flutist Herbie Mann on a Sony reel-to-reel tape player that our father sent me as a Christmas present. You embraced me on the sofa and comforted me and shared your own sadness and let me comfort you, as much as a child could. You helped me make sense of the move and believe that everything would get better as time progressed.

Thank you for your willingness to share your tears with me and make me feel older than my years. Thank you for all the assurances you provided that things would eventually work out. I wouldn't have made it through such a traumatic demarcation without you. You helped me take steps away from boyhood toward maturity. You helped me overcome a sense of disorientation and loss. You helped me learn to adapt to a vastly different world. I'm forever indebted to your sisterly love.

That was the closest we have ever been. Maybe one day we can be that close again.

CHAPTER 6:
Never Looking Back

DEAR MS. SANDRA KOLAK,

I entered the sixth grade after my family moved from Pennsylvania to California, casting me into a whirlwind of upheaval, loss, self-doubt, insecurity, and uncertainty. I felt as though the ground beneath me had shifted, and each step I took landed in such an unfamiliar, jagged place. The ground wasn't simply foreign; it seemed inhospitable. I was an outsider to others, but more importantly I felt like an outsider to myself. I wasn't comfortable in my own skin. Food didn't taste the same. The sun seemed to have taken a leave of absence. The perpetually dark, cloudy sky seemed to signal doom. I struggled to hang my clothes, insert my commas, and pedal my bike.

The move meant that I was leaving the secure, friendly confines of a small Catholic school and joining an enormous public campus with several sixth-grade classrooms and a swarm of busses and bungalows. I was introduced to games I was wholly ignorant of—kickball, tetherball, foursquare. I was coming from a sloped playground that facilitated games of tag on fair-weather days and rubber-soled shoe skiing through snow and on sheets of ice.

My western Pennsylvania dialect made me feel conspicuous and afraid to speak in my ethnically and linguistically diverse class. I had lost the guidance of my monsignor, priests, nuns, and extended family members, including grandparents, uncles, aunts, and cousins. The year was 1967 and my father had left for a year on a second tour of duty in Vietnam. I was living in a rental house too small for privacy with my mother, sister, and her husband. We were all grappling with disorientation and discomfort inherent in making the adjustment to new places and new ways.

I started the school year with a most disengaged, passive, seemingly uncaring teacher. To be fair, she was dealing with a major health issue, and she was replaced early in the year by a long-term substitute. The replacement teacher looked like a combination of Kim Novak and Grace Kelly, actresses I had seen in the films *Vertigo* and *Rear Window*. Needless to say, I was immediately enthralled, and my spirits were greatly lifted.

Far more consequential than your appearance, however, were your personality and approach to teaching. You quickly began to establish a personal, and at all times highly professional, relationship with your students. You asked questions about who we were as people, the lives we were living, our thoughts and feelings, dreams, fears, and aspirations. You did this by talking to us with great interest and empathy. You invited us to write about our lives. You had us get up in front of our classmates and deliver speeches on topics both personal and objective. You engaged us in art projects that were as much about our identity as they were about inspiring us to discover and express artistic talent, conveying our interests and preferred activities.

DEAR BOYS OF ALL SEASONS,

My happiest childhood memories that ignite the brightest flames are all set in a neighborhood park, the scene of sporting games from all seasons that brought together friends and neighborhood acquaintances who sought escape from parental control and opportunities to develop individual athleticism and experience esprit de corps.

At the time, of course, we were simply playing, letting our physical selves loose and making the most of every moment of sunlight, but with the perspective of age, I realize we were doing so much more than that.

How I would like to enjoy again the freedom from thought and worry those frequently planned and sometimes spontaneous games provided.

We took advantage of a long, wide expanse of grass to play a baseball game called "over the line." It required four players, but we could make it work with three if that's all we had. Ideally, the teams were two against two. You pitched underhand to your teammate—no base running necessary. With clothing or extra gloves, we defined an infield and outfield. We had the benefit of a chain link fence that served as a homerun wall. (Retrieving balls enabled me to foster efficient and safe fence-climbing skills.) Ground balls fielded cleanly were considered "outs." Ground balls past the infielder were "singles." Flies caught were "outs," of course. Balls fielded by the outfielder on the ground were "singles." Balls that rolled or bounced all the way to the fence were "doubles." A fly ball off the fence was a "triple." A ball over the fence was, of course, a homerun. We kept the imaginary base runners in our heads and tallied the runs scored after three outs.

For me, the sky has never looked so warm and welcoming as when I was tracking an arcing ball, using my glove to shield my eyes from the sun, and feeling the sting of the ball long after I had made my throw to my teammate. The out, mentally recorded, felt like an interest-bearing deposit in my emotional bank account.

In basketball season, we played half-court three-on-three games or full court if we had at least eight players. The nets were chain link and the backboards white plastic, but we loved them. If only two or three people gathered, we played "horse" or "pig."

We delighted in trick shots and performed our best imitations of Kareem Abdul-Jabbar's skyhook and Earl "the Pearl" Monroe's turn around jump shot. We called our own fouls and got ridiculed if we abused the practice. In our minds, we were running up and down the famous parquet floor in Boston Garden or the legend-varnished floorboards in Madison Square Garden. In our imagination, we went up against the likes of Bill Russell, Wilt Chamberlain, and Willis Reed. One moment I was Walt "Clyde" Frazier, the next Jerry (Zeke from Cabin Creek) West, and the next Oscar Robertson (the Big O). Ah, the fantasy of youth!

In fall and winter, we played tackle football. Even in our most competitive five-on-five games, where gang tackles were the norm, no one ever committed cheap shots. We made the plays while ensuring everyone's safety. We wanted to play on an endless string of tomorrows, and injuries would have been prohibitive. We instituted a three-second silent count before pass rushing, which guaranteed that exciting passing plays could develop. Our favorite games were played in the rain or just afterwards. We loved to slide in mud and didn't mind the wet clothing clinging to our bodies and weighing down our movements. It was part of our discipline.

I'm proud that we always divided up teams evenly based on height and weight. We wanted equitably matched games that would mean winning for either team was always possible.

A guy who lived across the street from our park would sometimes join our games. He was several years older than we were and much bigger and faster. To compensate for his age and skill advantage, we made special rules in football for him. We didn't have to tackle him; he was ruled "down" if we simply got two hands on his body. When he tackled us, he exhibited greatly appreciated restraint; otherwise, he could have done extreme bodily harm. In baseball, we moved home plate into another zip code. Our park bordered the 405 Freeway, and he could still hit a ball into traffic, a frightening display that he usually tried to avoid. In basketball, we let him go full throttle. Thankfully, his basketball skills paled in comparison to football and baseball abilities, so we needed no artificial advantage.

On idle days, my friends and I did backflips off the park's swing set, and late at night, we played hide-and-go-seek. My favorite place to hide was in grass hollows, dangerously exposed and relying on the cover of darkness, the ability to remain perfectly still, the discipline to barely breathe, and an unobservant seeker.

Those hours at the park were untethered to life's miseries. I'm forever indebted to my friends and companions who made those hours so enjoyable and memorable.

DEAR FATHER,

Although our relationship during my teenage years was fraught with awkwardness, tension, minor disagreements, and serious conflicts, the memory of your teaching me how to drive survives in stark contrast to all of our shared unhappiness. Reflecting a half-century later on those evenings after dinner when you would ask me if I wanted a driving lesson, I am filled with admiration for your patience, wisdom, and appreciation of your love and closeness.

For my lessons, we took full advantage of Golden West College's close proximity to our house and its large unpaved parking area. The campus had only been open for five years and building projects were ongoing. A parking area had been leveled but it still needed paving and lighting. At six in the evening, we found it deserted and a perfect place for me to practice turns, moving in reverse, and parallel parking between wooden posts that we kept in the trunk. The parking area was conveniently large and vacant, sufficient for me to accelerate to about fifty and then practice smooth braking.

I was about fourteen when we started our lessons, and by the time I enrolled in my high school's driver training course, I was a relatively experienced driver.

During our lessons, all of the awkwardness and tension between us melted away. I was receptive to your counsel, and you delivered it with a calm, nurturing, reassuring voice, quite the opposite from our typically harsh and strained daily interactions. I asked to continue our lessons, not so much for the actual instruction, but for the easy manner you displayed toward me, and the affectionate closeness we were uncharacteristically able to share.

A few weeks after I obtained my driver's license, I was second in line to exit a parking lot when the driver in front of me—behind the wheel of a station wagon with windows covered by curtains and the rear end elevated to an exaggerated height, common in 1972—backed into me rather than continuing to wait for an opening in traffic. He did so angrily and impatiently, gunning his engine and extensively pushing in the bumper and grill of your Plymouth Satellite. He was not much older than I was and blamed me for being in his way. In reality, his curtains obscured his view. I was nearly in a state of shock and shame for getting into an accident so soon after obtaining my license.

From a pay phone, I called you to let you know what had occurred. After describing the accident and fearing your reaction, you quietly and calmly asked, "Were you hurt in any way? Are you okay?" You asked nothing about the car until I had assured you that I was fine, just sorry and ashamed. You insisted that I had nothing to be sorry or ashamed about. Then you seized on the "teachable moment." You asked, "Do you think you can drive the car home? If you can, I want you to do so." I said I was afraid to drive after the accident. You said, "That's exactly why I want you to drive the car home. You cannot allow fear to overcome you."

The way that you responded to my phone call helped me understand that our disagreements and conflicts were unsubstantial and unimportant in the larger context of our relationship. Without directly saying "I love you," you let me know that you loved me unconditionally, and a son can ask no more of his father.

Thank you for the way you answered my phone call that night with such gentleness and an absence of disappointment, anger, or judgment. Thank you for insisting that I find the will to get back behind the wheel, controlling my fear rather than letting it control me. To this day, whenever I'm sitting behind a steering wheel, I always feel your presence and remember your lessons. My wheels are never far from that unpaved, unlit parking lot at Golden West College. You are forever next me in every car, on every road, keeping me safe with your gentle, wise voice.

DEAR DAVID BOND,

We sat in twenty-four-hour coffee shops as high school students, drinking coffee and eating bear claws. That was how we spent many of our Friday or Saturday nights while others were out drinking, cruising, dating, avoiding pressing questions about the future, and having fun. If we had had invitations or opportunities to do the same, we would have accepted them. That's not intended as a self-pitying statement; it's simply a reality. Truth be told, we did those things occasionally, but more often than not, we met in one of three or four nearby coffee shops and talked like confused teenagers and tired old men. We relied on waitresses to refill our cups and to tolerate our extended encampments in their booths. We tried to compensate for our meager tabs at the end of the night with generous tips.

I'm thankful that you accepted all of my teenage angst with such loyal friendship and good humor. I hope I did the same for you. How embarrassed I'm sure I'd be today if I could listen to our conversations. I'm glad my memory is not that exact. The important point is that you always answered my phone calls when I suggested we meet. I know that I always tried to answer yours.

I have a clear memory that you would sit perfectly still and silent whenever I would tell a stupid joke or try to make a witty comment. For several seconds you debated in your mind whether to laugh or not. You would keep steady eye contact and I would return your look, imploring you without words to laugh. After your internal deliberation, you usually ended up laughing, perhaps more as a release of your indecision than an acknowledgement of my humor or wit. Thank you for that. Your laughter, regardless of its impetus, was encouraging, affirming, and invigorating. It made the coffee taste better, the lights less garish, and the future more hopeful.

As we sat together, we were working hard to figure out who we were and who we wanted to become. We observed the other patrons, fearing that we were seeing older versions of ourselves. The elderly couples seemed especially frail and vulnerable, but also adorable. We respected their longevity and loyalty. The middle-aged couples seemed exhausted by life, frequently overrun with mischievous children. The dating couples always seemed to consist of a strikingly beautiful girl and a guy we thought didn't deserve her. We were unreasonably judgmental and a bit jealous. Mostly, we were scared that the future would be unfulfilling. We tried to drown our typical teenage angst with cup after cup of coffee.

For a few hours, on those nights, we simultaneously tried to shut out the world and to make sense of it. I hope I'm not being hyperbolic to think that we created a much-needed refuge for each other. I can think of no better definition of friendship.

On Saturday mornings, we met friends to play three-on-three basketball. You and I always matched up based on our same height.

Our friends believed in setting teams that were evenly matched to ensure competitive games. I'm proud of that. We each played hard to win, but we shunned an "at any cost" philosophy. We knew that winning without lopsided advantages would mean more.

Guarding you was endlessly challenging. Your natural athleticism far exceeded mine. You possessed stunning vertical leaping ability. You were an unselfish player with supreme passing prowess, but you could shoot and score whenever you wanted to, like Oscar Robertson. I relished the experience of guarding you and trying to score against you. Your skills made me a better player. I learned to work harder to compensate for lesser skills. I learned to appreciate and celebrate someone else's talent. I learned how to press myself to squeeze out every ounce of desire and effort. I learned how to make myself better by playing against someone better than I was. I learned my place in the food chain and how to avoid using my lower-than-preferred ranking as an excuse.

Thank you for all the refuge you afforded me through the perils of teenage anguish. Thank you for giving me an opportunity to discover the value of desire and heart in human endeavors.

DEAR MS. KAREN FRIEDRICH,

We were confused teenagers, searching for our voices, desperate to be heard, not really knowing where to begin our stories, not really sure if we even had stories to tell.

You were our English teacher, on a mission to bring Advanced Placement courses to our school that didn't have any until you pushed, pulled, insisted, guilt-tripped, and advocated. We knew nothing of your struggles except what you hinted at and what you let slip through your battle fatigue and emotional wounds. You were a strong female in a still male-dominated world, and you had to fight through lingering sexism that had been exposed and put on the defensive in the 1960s, but was far from eradicated in the early 1970s.

You knew that we could only discover our stories and find our voices by reading the best literature that you dared put into our hands: Hermann Hesse, John Updike, Jimmy Breslin, Edith Wharton, Willa Cather, Joan Didion, Virginia Woolf, Norman Mailer, John Dos

Passos, Ernest Hemingway, Mark Twain, and Sinclair Lewis, to name a few.

You described horizons for us, but you wisely knew we had to create our own. Great literature was your medicine; you were a doctor writing prescriptions. You were intent on developing our powers of introspection while simultaneously enlarging our capacity to express our minds and hearts with as much eloquence as a teenage mind is capable of.

So many of your colleagues were instead shoveling information as if we were cavernous holes that needed filling. How much dirt could we absorb? How much dirt would we allow to settle without tossing it out or rearranging it in fits of claustrophobia?

You, on the other hand, would stroll by our desks and shyly place books on the corners, challenging us to open your gifts to discover not only what lay within, but more importantly to uncover what pulsated truly and defiantly in our hearts and minds.

Thank you for the enlightenment you so bravely shared with us and the self-discoveries you made possible.

CHAPTER 11:
Sock Hops

DEAR JOAN,

Is it pathetic or endearing to be infatuated with an almost girlfriend from high school fifty years later? To consciously revive this memory says what exactly about my outlook as a sixty-six-year-old man? Am I admitting that the past entices me more than the future? Am I holding on to a memory from youth as a way to stave off thoughts of mortality? Or am I simply mining a memory from a period when so much of my identity was yet to be formed, and I was reaching out for connections and testing boundaries to help shape my uncertain steps?

While I ponder these questions, I take delight in seeing you sitting alone in the bleachers at a Friday night post-football game dance, called sock hops in that fading 1970s era. Shy and timid, I spent most of my time in that setting walking around the gym, trying to look as though I had someplace to go, someone to meet, when in fact I was just trying to blend in and not look conspicuous.

Thankfully, there was always a crush of bodies to weave my way through: students who were entering and exiting the gym (innocent times back then; security measures hardly necessary); students who were dancing with a defined partner, usually to the music of a live band; students like me who were trying to look like they belonged; students huddled in groups conversing about music and politics (Nixon and McGovern were such magnetic figures regardless of one's preferences); students who were content to watch and listen to the band, calling out song requests and boldly singing along in appreciation of the band's accommodations.

Sometimes you were sitting alone and sometimes you were with a friend. You always seemed to sit in the same place, about three-quarters of the way up into the wooden bleachers, off to one side and partly in the shadows. From that perch you had a great vantage point on all the proceedings playing out on the gym floor. Not many students sat in the bleachers, so you were able to stretch your legs and recline.

We were acquaintances but not friends. Occasionally we were in the same classes, but our connection never progressed beyond shy greetings. At the sock-hops, I always kept an eye out for you. I was aware if you were on the gym floor dancing or sitting in the bleachers.

I spent considerable energy summoning the nerve to approach you to ask you to dance. I think I tried to expend my endless reserves of nervous energy by circling the gym floor before approaching you. I was so shy, so inexperienced, so uncertain, and so self-conscious. You were so graceful, so nonjudgmental, so understanding. I wonder if you observed my apprehension, if you were aware of how much time and effort I wasted in getting up the nerve to approach you?

I am eternally grateful for your welcoming smile, for always saying "yes" to my invitation to dance, for accepting my shyness, for tolerating my awkwardness, for being patient and forcing nothing, for not laughing at my inept dance moves, and for allowing me to hold you tightly through the slow songs, guiding my unsure hands.

All these years later, whenever I hear "Your Song" by Elton John or "A Whiter Shade of Pale" by Procol Harum, I can feel your warm, supple body against mine. I can feel the two of us swaying gently, lost in our own world, free of shyness, inhibitions, uncertainty, if only for a few songs, for a few evenings.

Thank you for all your patience and tenderness.

PART TWO: GRANDPARENTS

CHAPTER 12:
A Menu of Love

DEAR MATERNAL GRANDMOTHER,

Words were not an integral part of our relationship. I knew you through your physical acts of love and kindness, and through the oddities of your old and worn three-story structure that constituted a house in the most fascinating and mysterious way.

You were a Russian immigrant, following your husband in the early twentieth century via Canada to a small western Pennsylvania town named Charleroi, where he had found work in a Corning glass factory. Both of you were illegals in your adopted country for much of your lives. Your husband lived in fear that one day he would be picked up and sent back to your motherland, Ukraine.

Meanwhile, you raised five kids in a five-room house, worshiped in a Russian Orthodox church, played bingo on Friday nights at your church, and on Saturday nights often carried your drunken husband over your shoulder from your ground-floor back door up a dangerously steep flight of stairs to a makeshift second-floor bedroom. Your steps lacked depth to support more than half of your foot as you climbed, and how you never stumbled or dropped your husband is eternally inscrutable.

I suspect that you knew more English than you let on, and you kept your secret well disguised with your accent and ungrammatical, broken speech. "Oh, you probly hungry. Sit down. I cook for you. It ready in a minute." You would then turn to your wood-burning, cast-iron stove—that to my young eyes had the weight and dimensions of a tank—and use it to produce heavy, delicious meals of cabbage, kielbasa, and perogies. Everything dripped with the flavor of onion and oil. You had your cheap, plastic radio sitting atop your refrigerator and tuned to a station that played Russian music all through the day and night and broadcast Russian mass on Sundays.

Your husband died when I was quite young, so most of my memories of you are when you were a widow. I do have a vibrant memory of my grandfather going into the cellar to cut a bothersome mole off his forearm with a penknife. He returned to the kitchen, bleeding, and you bandaged him up like a field nurse, tearing up a cloth napkin and cutting tape with your teeth, lathering Mercurochrome with a slightly sadistic grin. You scolded him like a mother would scold a child. "Why you do dat? That mole was 'na-ting' to you. Leave things like dat alone for your own good."

Years later, you accepted your husband's passing with heroic stoicism. "He was a good man and he said goodbye too early."

Sleepovers at your house promised nights of intrigue and adventure. I shared your bed and lay perfectly still as you relieved yourself in the middle of the night with a bedpan. Your house had one bathroom, up a second steep flight of stairs on the third floor, in my aunt's bedroom. In your ground-floor cellar you had a toilet and a rustic laundry sink, so your bedpan got a lot of use.

Before you went to sleep you would wind up an oversized alarm clock that you used more out of habit than need. You always gave in to my desire to wind it up for you. You always checked and affirmed my work. "Dat's good."

In winter, you got up in the middle of the night to shovel coal into your coal-burning stove that sat in the middle of your cellar, off the kitchen through an imposing, thick wooden door. I would get up with you and shadow your effort. Sometimes you had to open another door that led to a coal storage room. I loved to help you, and you tolerated my interference with your process. You had to shovel coal twice each night to keep the poorly insulated house warm, and I loved helping you, though in reality I'm afraid I was more of a nuisance. Still, you never objected to my desire to help.

Until you were in your late eighties, you resisted attempts by your sons and daughters to replace your coal-burning stove with a modern, gas-burning unit. "Why I need dat for? My stove's plenty good." You finally relented, but you always said you missed your old furnace.

On Friday nights, I would walk with you to your church and sit with you while you played bingo. You played several cards at once and freely complained as you lost game after game. "These cards no good."

Without a driver's license, much less a car, you walked everywhere you went, including the grocery store, which fortunately was less than a mile away. I loved to accompany you, pushing the cart that you kept just outside your backyard gate. I was always anxious to witness your interactions with the butcher. You would hold a package of meat in your calloused hands as if you had evidence of some great injustice. You would seek out the butcher and make your appeal. "Why is dis meat so much? I should pay half dat." The butcher would always smile and gently respond, "I don't set the price. I just cut it up and package it. I'm sorry, Mrs. Popovich." You usually dropped the package back into the display case with a shrug and a smile. "I no pay dat price. I come back when it's lower." Together we wheeled the cart back to your house, our arms vibrating as the cart bounced wildly over the brick streets and the trolley tracks.

I loved sitting next to you on your back porch glider. You padded it with several blankets to make it quite cozy and comfortable. The extra padding was especially welcome in the colder months. You gently moved the glider back and forth to my delight when my feet couldn't reach the ground. When my feet did reach the wooden floorboards, I kept pace with your gliding motion. We would look out at your garden that took up all the space of your sloping backyard. We watched the rain; we gazed at the Monongahela River that all your kids swam in when they were growing up.

You tended your lush garden by hauling buckets of water to and from the spigot on the side of your house. I don't recall ever seeing a hose. You maintained your garden literally until the day you died, which we estimate to have been around the age of ninety-five. Your birth certificate was lost on your journey by ship from one side of the world to another when you were a young married woman forever altering the course of her life.

You spent virtually all of your adult life at your house. You went only to places within walking distance: church and grocery and neighbors' houses to visit on the front porches. You cared for my aunt Mary, your spinster daughter, nearly all of her life, waking her in the morning, preparing her breakfast, putting together her brown-bag lunch, often with an overdose of Saran wrap that frustrated her to no end, and cooking her dinner. You did your laundry in an old-fashioned wringer washing machine and hung the clothes outside in spring and summer and inside the cellar in fall and winter. You could not bend an index finger after smashing it between the rollers. I don't think you ever went anywhere by car, and I know you never traveled by train or plane.

In the evening, you sat in your yellow recliner in front of your beloved TV set, watching Lawrence Welk, local news, and game shows. You read a Russian-language newspaper and smiled every time your cuckoo clock sounded, the tiny bird always tickling your fancy.

When you died, you left me a little money, just enough to pay for my roundtrip plane ticket from San Francisco to Pittsburgh in order to attend your funeral. In death, your stout body looked lighter than air. I thought you were going to float out of the casket. The skin on your face was soft like roses and wrinkle-free. Any doubts that we have souls were erased as I looked at your body. It became undeniably clear to me that your soul had left your body, causing your appearance of lightness.

Blessed Eva Popovich, you were one of the happiest people I have ever known. Even in death you looked happy. You expressed your love through small acts of kindness and generosity, which through the years have grown ever larger and more profound.

DEAR PATERNAL GRANDMOTHER,

You were a woman of few words and many loving gestures. You communicated mostly through your humble nature and the food you prepared for others. You always had a large pot of homemade marinara sauce simmering on the stove. You always had freshly baked bread rising in the oven. You stood patiently and lovingly by my side as I broke open your bread, let the steam warm my face, and dipped a piece into your thick sauce, making me feel like a lucky conspirator.

Most of the time, you were reclusive, remaining on your feet in the kitchen as your immediate and extended family indulged in your traditional after-church Sunday feast: the fruit and vegetables came from your garden; the soup was profoundly simple and indescribably delicious—subtle chicken broth, pastina, parsley, celery, and seasonings that even your daughters couldn't easily explain. The tables were covered with eggplant, spareribs, chicken, spaghetti, lasagna, ravioli, artichokes, delectable cheeses, and assorted Italian cuts of meat that I couldn't pronounce or spell, such as prosciutto, capocollo, pancetta, and porchetta.

In the evenings, you sat on your front or back porch, with your feet crossed, gently rocking or gliding back and forth. When it was cold, you wrapped a shawl around your shoulders, but still insisted on staying outdoors for part of the day, even when it rained or snowed. Your gaze always seemed to be on something indistinct that you never felt a need to comment on. Even inside when you were sitting with others on the couch, your eyes never seemed to land on the TV or others in the room. Your face betrayed no emotion; you kept your thoughts to yourself.

You seemed happy to exile your husband to his chicken coop a good distance from your house, and you called him "a dirty old man" when he would invariably try to slice watermelon with a rusty, bloody machete that he used to slaughter chickens.

Your husband was from southern Italy, impoverished Calabria. You were from northern Italy, used to refinement and culture. Yet somehow you two found each other. Family lore said that when you saw him, you knew he was "the one," despite his humble origin. You gave up a sophisticated life to marry a man from a different social and economic class, have your first of eight children, and make the uncertain journey to America at the turn of the twentieth century.

In a western Pennsylvania steel and coal town, you created a world for yourself centered on family, kitchen, garden, church, and the hucksters that facilitated social gatherings on your street and convenient shopping for meat and vegetables.

You were oh-so-stoic and mysterious.

I think your garden was your real church. You bent to the soil with reverence and carried your harvests into the house with strong yet delicate hands and solemn steps.

I apologize for my part in desecrating your garden with cousins and boys from the neighborhood by engaging in elaborate tomato fights. We lined up in two opposing rows of warriors, arming ourselves with the green tomatoes that had fallen off the vines, then hurling them with all the force and accuracy we could muster, wearing the evidence of our battle on our clothing like proud combatants, thoughtlessly inciting your disappointment and wrath. You chased us away with a broom or shovel, scolding us in fluent Italian and broken English.

On sleepovers with my cousins, we would usually stay up till the wee hours, make too much noise, and wake you. You would walk partway down the steep wooden steps that led from the main floor where your bedroom was located to the cellar where we were camping out to scold us. You would typically mutter something in Italian and leave us with the words, "Oy, yoy yoy yoy yoy yoy" echoing in our guilty ears.

I don't think I ever had a conversation with you that went beyond thanking you for letting me stay in your house and of course for the delicious food that you lovingly served. You always greeted me and said goodbye with a stiff hug, and you let me kiss you on the cheek, but I don't think you really wanted the human touch.

How I wish I could go back in time and ask you what it was like to cross an ocean by ship with a young child in your arms, plant roots in foreign soil, and make do while your husband walked home from his job in the steel mill where he labored as a "hotshot" bricklayer, quickly rebuilding the furnaces that melted from intense heat. Eventually, he saved up enough money to build you a proper house that you spent the rest of your life in, raising five sons and two daughters. You stoically endured the loss of one child to the flu pandemic in 1918 and an adult son to ALS.

Thank you, dearest Mary Coccari, for creating a setting for me that was a second home, where I would learn about the world from listening to all the family conversations—sometimes comical, sometimes prosaic, and sometimes internecine—while eating the most delightful food imaginable. How I wish I could have known your thoughts and heard your life stories, as you stood apart in the kitchen, refilling platters of food, never quite making eye contact with your progeny.

PART THREE: UNCLES

CHAPTER 14:
A Model of Contentment

DEAR UNCLE FRANK,

Thank you for always being such a rock of integrity, stability, grace, and humility. You were one of the people in my life whose temperament and manner taught me more about how to conduct myself than words ever could. I haven't always lived up to your standard of tranquil emotional equilibrium, but I have always held that standard close to my heart, and I have tried to follow your illustrious example of a life well lived.

As the husband of one of my father's sisters, you found yourself in the midst of never-ending drama: family gossip, petty and substantial conflicts, much vociferous arguing about nothing and everything, occasional bloodletting, the harboring of real and imagined grievances, and decades-long feuds.

You calmly occupied a sturdy, neutral position in the eye of the family storms that swirled corrosively and encompassed everyone else. You were always the man with the calm voice and unflinching eye, seeking to de-escalate, to put things in perspective not with words but by celebrating life's simple pleasures: a strong cup of coffee, a second slice of pie, a leisurely stroll through the garden after dinner, an unperturbed posture on a porch swing.

You never took a side in family disputes; you never judged, ridiculed, patronized, or rejected. Instead, you supported, sought the silver lining, reminded people of their humanity, served others before yourself, extended your magnanimity to all, tried to imbue others with your sense of goodwill, and to your core felt true contentment with a simple life free of internal conflict.

You were a man at peace with yourself and the world. You never let life diminish the lustrous twinkle in your eyes, erase the genuine smile from your face, erode your belief in God, or weaken your enjoyment of simply being alive.

Growing up, I was obsessed with and fascinated by your silver-white hair. It was fluffy like fresh snow, though sometimes you stiffened it with something oily. As a child, you let me crawl close to you, pull your ever-present comb out of your shirt pocket, and first muss and then comb your hair over and over again. You sat perfectly still, letting me destroy your hair's perfect part and then try clumsily to restore it. Never once did you deny me this annoying indulgence. How easy it would have been for you to hide your comb or simply tell me, "Not today." Instead, you always smiled, gave me your lap freely, and permitted and endured my silliness.

I fondly recall many outings you and Aunt Lena treated my cousins and me to. In the summer you would drive the three of us to a miniature golf/arcade locale called Sweeny's. While we cavorted through the golf course and played in the arcade, you patiently sat in your Chrysler Imperial and listened to your beloved Pittsburgh Pirates baseball games on the radio. You never complained about our selfish dawdling; you never minded the suffocating Pennsylvania humidity. You graciously provided us with blessed freedom in a small town that offered its youth little in the way of recreational outlets.

These excursions usually began with a delicious breaded shrimp dinner at the restaurant next door. At the table, you indulged us with Roy Roger's beverages with extra cherries, and you interacted with us as if we were adults, never patronizing or suffocating in the way that our fathers sometimes were, pouncing on every immature gesture or syllable. In your presence, we could breathe and express ourselves. We loved you for that and so much more.

How I loved to spend the night at my grandmother's house, where you also resided, and listen from my sofa bed as you had breakfast and prepared to leave for your job in the steel mill. You sat at the table drinking coffee and enjoying toast with the contentment of a king sitting on his throne, contemplating a vast empire. But humility was your aura. I sneaked looks when you thought I was asleep and studied your joy, happiness, and peaceful disposition. You considered each day a personal gift from God, apprehending it slowly and patiently, savoring its beauty and charm.

On Sundays at noon mass in St. Cajetan's Catholic Church, you fulfilled your duties as usher with profound faith, devotion, and humility. Your steady hands extended the collection basket as if you were delivering a baby. You were the embodiment of sacred, gentle care, and reverence.

Late in life, with your wife deceased and the end near for you, I watched you sitting at a bus stop, talking animatedly with a few peers, aged men who loved to tell stories. You relaxed on that wooden bench for hours as if it were a luxurious sofa, letting the buses come and go. You were exactly where you wanted to be.

Thank you for your kindness, your tolerance, your generosity of time, your peaceful presence in a family that thrived on disagreement, dissension, and conflict. Thank you for your example of equanimity and gratitude in a family desperately in need of it.

DEAR UNCLE LOU,

I could tell by the way my father acted in your presence how deeply he respected you. You were his older brother and that would have been enough to warrant the deference he displayed to you. But you also had earned a college degree, something my father lacked, and I think he valued your degree more than you did. But on the deepest level, my father considered you a paragon of decency, integrity, decorum, and intelligence.

Your parents didn't have the financial means to send more than one son to college, and that honor was reserved for you. My father felt slighted, but he never held that against you or his parents. He accepted his fate and found another way, first through the steel mill and then in the US Army.

My father was never envious of your entitlement, and the admiration he felt for you was conveyed in every conversation the two of you had. My father deferred to few people, and then usually with great struggle and tongue biting, even in the military chain of command. But I could always detect his esteem for you in his body language and tone. You were his superior in age and education, and he revered your status in all matters. I witnessed this and followed his example.

You returned his respect by treating me with extraordinary kindness and concern. You would go out of your way to take me on excursions to our downtown G. C. Murphy's Five and Dime store to buy me toys.

In the car, you sang songs to me that you made up on the spot. "There once was a boy named Mike/Who couldn't figure out what he liked/He sat on his bike/Like a regular tyke/And sometimes went for a hike." I was enthralled by your skills of improvisation.

In the store, you strolled around patiently, giving me space and time as I examined everything before making a selection. You put no restrictions on cost, but I honored the way my father always honored you by keeping my choices modest.

Dressed in your crisp white shirt, meticulously tied tie, pressed slacks, and light jacket, you held your arms behind your back and walked the crowded aisles as if you were on vacation. You were such a figure of dignity and integrity. I can still hear your melodic whistling, letting me know that you were in no hurry and that you were close by. You made me feel quite special, and I tried to convey my thanks and appreciation by showing you the same degree of deference and respect that my father exhibited.

I have fond memories of you and Aunt Theresa, your wife, coming to our house on countless early evenings for pie and coffee. Aside from the time you spent at your parents' house, these visits were your primary social outlet. You would sit at our kitchen table for an hour or two, sipping coffee and indulging in my mother's homemade apple, peach, or berry pie with ice cream. You talked about the extended Coccari family with great compassion and reviewed my progress in school.

Many years later, I found out that for more than a year you and my father were not on speaking terms. There was a dispute over money that my father had sent monthly to your parents during his first few years in the military. My father insisted that he sent $100 faithfully, and you said there was no record of such payments. You kept the financial records for my grandparents, and my father simply wanted acknowledgement of his assistance. He was not looking for recompense, only recognition. The matter remained unresolved.

During this period when the two of you were not speaking, you still came to our house a few times a week for coffee and pie. At the table, the conversation flowed, so no one knew you were both waging your own private wars of silence when otherwise alone. I never saw evidence that my father ever allowed his respect for you to weaken. Eventually, you allowed the dispute to be washed away by healing time and resumed talking privately. Many years later, my father showed me letters he had written to you, vociferously arguing his side, but always with the utmost love and veneration.

From my mother, I learned that when the two of you were growing up, you fought like brothers often do, wrestling and throwing punches, tearing clothing and leaving marks. But the competition was always overshadowed by my father's admiration for you.

When my family left our hometown in Pennsylvania for California, your goodbye to me was especially fraught with emotion and trauma. You embraced me as I had never been embraced before or since. You trembled as you hugged me and wept into my body for an interminable period. You heightened the sorrow I felt at leaving exponentially by the way you couldn't let go. At the time, I was afraid, and only many years later did I understand that that was your way of returning all the respect my father had rendered to you.

When you died from stomach cancer at age sixty-five, the devastation my father experienced was ever present. He marked the important dates of your life on his calendars every year until he died: your birthday, your death day, your discharge from the Army, and your date of marriage. While it is true that my father marked his calendars in this way for many family members, your dates elicited in him a particularly deep feeling of sadness. I cannot count the number of times that my father would express his sadness over your death by cursing out loud, "Son of a bitch. Lou was taken too soon." Sometimes I would find him sitting at his desk at home, looking at your photograph, flipping through the artifacts of your life that he carefully kept in a file folder, fighting back tears.

Thank you for being a hero to my father. Thank you for all the kindness, tenderness, sage advice, and love you freely and generously gave to me.

CHAPTER 16:
A Man I Wanted to Know Better

DEAR UNCLE BOB,

I knew you quite superficially when I was growing up. You were distant not only with me but with the entire family. Your house was next door to your parents', but on Sundays when the immediate and extended family gathered for the traditional after-mass meal, you usually stayed at home and your wife fixed you a plate and took it over to you. The excuse was always the same, "Bob's tired from the station [your gas station] and he's resting." My memory is void of even one occasion when you joined everyone.

To be fair to you, your Atlantic-Richfield (later known simply as ARCO) full-service station was an incredibly demanding enterprise. Through all the years before self-service, you maintained loyal customers by not only pumping gas but also cleaning windshields, checking oil levels, tire air pressure, and anything else the regulars requested. You performed this service through Pennsylvania's debilitating humidity in summer and single-digit snow and sleet storms in winter. You also repaired vehicles in your two-bay garage. I remember your hands and nails were always marred by grease and oil. Your station opened at sunrise and closed at midnight. Trustworthy help, always hard to come by, meant you had to be on the premises for both opening and closing, so your work hours were brutal.

When I was in fourth and fifth grades, my father would sometimes let me spend a few hours at your station. But you never let me work alongside your first son, who is a few years older than I am. I desperately wanted to help out, but out of respect for my father, you wouldn't dare let me get my clothes or hands dirty. Instead, you gave me dimes to use in your soda machine, a shiny red refrigerator with a skinny vertical window showing the soda bottles lined up like soldiers. I drank Mountain Dew and shadowed my cousin, getting as close as I could to him while he cleaned windshields and fixed tire leaks. You wanted to deliver me back to my father in the exact condition in which I had been dropped off. I loved those hours at your station, watching you inspect the undercarriage of cars and use all manner of tools to conduct repairs. I was fascinated by your single-pole rotary airlifts that enabled you to raise the vehicles off the ground high enough for you to stand under and perform inspections and needed repairs. For a kid, standing beneath two raised cars and pretending to be a mechanic was so much better than any fort made of pillows, sofa cushions, and sheets.

When you lost your wife to a terminal disease after three decades of marriage, you were a model of stoicism and strength. My memory is seared with an image of you and Aunt Betty sitting on a blanket at a community picnic. You looked like teenagers happily ensconced in your own world. At my young age, I could not articulate that your souls were permanently intertwined, but I could sense the unbreakable connection that you shared. After your wife's death, I stood in awe of how you endured. She had been your partner for virtually all of your adult life, and you had to find a way to carry on for some four decades afterwards.

As an adult, I had an opportunity to spend a few days with you while visiting my hometown. I feel that was when I began to know you just a little after years of distance and mystery. I had returned to the US from two years of teaching English in Japan. You were a paratrooper in WWII and to you the Japanese were a forever enemy. You were baffled that I had traveled there, and you were surprised to hear me compliment the Japanese people for their kindness, graciousness, and hospitality. You knew them under very different circumstances, and you could not reconcile any evolution in their attitude toward America and its citizens. Nonetheless, we had a great time talking about the family and our respective life experiences. I remember you lamenting the transition ARCO forced on you from operating a full-service station to self-serve. The change caused you to lose connection to your customers and made the business purely transactional and thereby quite sterile. Opportunities for human touch, sadly lost.

I thanked you for the hours I spent at your service station, and also for letting me sit in your living room as a kid, while you stretched out on the sofa, resting from your grueling hours at your work, and watching late-night war movies. On those evenings, you were distant and introspective, but always exuding a "live and let live" respect toward me.

I miss your stoicism and strength. I wish I could have known you better.

DEAR UNCLE ERNIE,

My thank you to you will be easily interpreted as sarcastic and impertinent. While this letter is undeniably impertinent, buried deep in my sarcasm exists a morsel of sincere thanks for being an example of the kind of man I did not want to grow up to be. I could have gotten here without you, and would have preferred doing so, but I suppose the benefits of your negative example outweigh the costs if I put enough effort into the assessment.

As the eldest son in my father's family, you used your exalted status to abuse and exploit your mother shamelessly and caused your brothers to disparage you behind your back (my father to your face).

In many ways, you were the proverbial big fish in a small pond, and you played that role for all it was worth. At its zenith, our hometown's population barely exceeded 20,000. Monessen, Pennsylvania, built along the Monongahela River about twenty miles southeast of Pittsburgh, was a diverse community of immigrants, including Italian, Russian, Polish, and Greek, among others, who pursued the American Dream in steel mills, coal mines, factories, and mom-and-pop main street stores.

By virtue of your firstborn male status, you inherited a relatively small Chrysler-Plymouth-Dodge dealership from your father's brother. It was a two-story structure with a showroom barely large enough for two vehicles, a modest garage, a decrepit auto parts area, and a tiny, sooty second-story apartment occupied through the years by various family members. My parents and sister lived there for a time prior to my birth.

In the 1950s when you inherited the dealership, the mills, mines, factories, and retail stores were all burning hot with activity. Our hometown was a microcosm of the country's economic and middle class expansion. The dealership was primed for enlargement. Property close by was available at bargain-basement rates, which would have enabled you to increase inventory and operations. But you kept the dealership to yourself like a petulant child, unwilling to share it, squandering growth and expansion in the process. Your three brothers, including my father, begged you to allow them to join you, not as part owners, but simply as employees. My uncle Bob was interested in developing his skills as an auto mechanic, but you wouldn't give him a chance to do so in your dealership. He went to work for his father-in-law, who owned a small auto repair shop, and learned his trade outside of your influence or support. My uncle Lou would have been perfect to oversee sales. He was the one brother who had the benefit of a college degree, and he had the capacity to develop strategic marketing and business plans. But you wouldn't let him in. My father begged you to let him run the auto parts operation. He pushed you hard to acquire additional property to facilitate expansion. But you rebuffed him as if his ideas were insane.

It's pointless to speculate on what might have occurred if you had welcomed your brothers into the business. But it is a tragedy that you selfishly and parsimoniously shut the door on their familial loyalty, capacity for hard work, talents, and ideas. You behaved like a fat king, unwilling to budge from his disintegrating throne.

Eventually, the city bought your dealership in order to tear it down and widen roads. No one knows how much money you made, but estimates were in the hundreds of thousands of dollars.

Despite your relative wealth, you lived nearly all your life in a house you rented from your mother. You paid a ridiculously small amount in rent, and relied on your mother to pay for everything from a replacement light bulb to a new roof and everything in between. I nearly saw you and my father come to physical blows over your stinginess. When your mother died, you moved into her home without any thought of sharing it with your siblings.

Your miserliness was matched by your arrogance and thoughtlessness. On Sundays after noon Mass, our large family congregated at your mother's for an early dinner. People were seated by 1:30, enjoying soup, spaghetti, chicken, vegetables grown in your mother's garden, and homemade sauce and bread. Everyone— including your three brothers, two sisters, in-laws, nieces, nephews, cousins, and sometimes friends—except you.

After dinner was over and the dishes washed and put away, you made a grand entrance around 3 or sometimes later. Your mother had to serve you separately, starting the whole process over again. You conducted yourself like royalty; in your mind, I suppose your firstborn status entitled you to such indulgence. The rest of the family wept for what you forced your mother to endure. On occasions when my father confronted you, your mother objected and came to your defense. Other family members questioned my father's temerity and shunned him. Only he paid a price; you skated free. When your mother died, of course you inherited her house. Despite your relative wealth, you never bought a home of your own with your own money.

As a child, I gathered my knowledge of you from my parents, aunts, and uncles. I suppose you had a side to your history, but I cannot imagine how you could possibly justify your behaviors. Perhaps that is my shortcoming, but I'll live with it.

I recall a few occasions when you would visit my mother and me when my father's military career kept him away. You would sit for an hour or two at our kitchen table and drink coffee with my mother. My mother didn't drive, and she had to rely on the bus to make trips to the grocery store or doctor's office. Never once did you offer to give her a ride for such errands or appointments.

During your visit, you would usually ask me if I wanted to play catch with you in our backyard. From about ninety feet away, your pencil-thin mustache and wiry hair looked especially dastardly, like some villain in a silent movie. I would throw the ball as hard as I could, wanting to make your hand sting till you couldn't stand it and would call an end to our game of catch. It was my way of getting a bit of retribution. I'm not sorry for it.

After my family had moved to California and your dealership had been torn down and paved over by the boulevard expansion project, we would make cross-country trips in the summer to visit all our relatives. I recall you taking me into a single car garage that you used to house a dealer-plated, leftover Chrysler. You were preserving all its pristine chrome and paint and leather. You had it covered with a car bag and you carefully removed it as if you were about to reveal some priceless historical artifact or piece of artwork. You expected me to fawn over the car, to be enchanted by its newness, and to marvel at the single digit odometer reading. Your pride was more suffocating than the dark, cramped garage. "I never drive it," you assured me, as if that were some badge of honor. Apparently, you kept the car as you kept your dealership, under tight wraps.

You would then command me to follow you to an office you kept downtown that bore the name "Coccari Garage" that used to front your dealership. You had two oversized wooden desks occupying the constricted office space, making it nearly impossible to walk around. I was expected to genuflect at the surviving evidence of your dealership. To you, I imagine the Chrysler in your garage and the moribund office space were testaments to your proud inheritance and profit. To me, they were symbols of what might have been.

I know all too well how deeply my father was tormented by your inexplicable treatment of the mother you shared. You took full advantage of her love, loyalty, generosity, and passivity.

Until the day he died, my father lamented the way you shut out other family members from the career and economic possibilities the car dealership could have provided. My father believed that the dealership could have been developed into a major enterprise that would have made life a little easier for the entire family. But you chose to keep it for yourself, sadly letting it falter and wane until the city fortuitously bailed you out.

Yet I also know that my father loved you through all your selfishness and exploitation. You were his older brother, and he looked up to you. He never stopped needing you to be a better role model for him.

In his file cabinet, my father kept newspaper clippings documenting your work as a champion of our hometown's redevelopment projects. He also documented your moonlighting as an accomplished clarinet and saxophone player in a well-respected nightclub band that over the years performed with Sammy Davis Jr., Liberace, Vic Damone, and many other top-line performers. In the eyes of the community, you were a local hero and celebrity.

In a prominent place in his den, my father kept a picture of the two of you in middle age, shoulder to shoulder, blood brothers forever.

Thank you, Uncle Ernie, for being my definitive incarnate symbol of how not to act as a son or sibling, and for providing me with a cautionary tale of what might have been. Thank you for reminding me to be cognizant of my father's consummate example of unconditional, undying brotherly love and devotion. Thank you for providing me the opportunity to appreciate the way my father proceeded when his dream was thwarted by your greed and selfishness.

DEAR UNCLE JOHN,

You were always such an enigmatic, fascinating figure to me when I was growing up. As my mother's youngest of three brothers, I encountered you on a few occasions during visits to my grandmother's house. You immediately captured my attention with the bolt-action rifle you kept in a corner of the bedroom you shared with your brothers growing up, its scope bold and shiny and its wood grains well oiled. I was forbidden to touch it, an admonition I never violated, but I sure gazed at it for long stretches with equal parts wonder and fear. I want to thank you for bringing such intrigue and mystery to my relatively sheltered life.

All that I knew about you I learned from my parents. You dropped out of high school and enlisted in the Navy, choosing military service over school, as many young Americans did when the US entered WWII. You were all of sixteen and altered your identification papers in order to enlist.

After the war, you became a merchant seaman and spent your life on ships traveling around the world, mostly to Hong Kong and Vietnam.

When you were between assignments on ships, you were in San Francisco or Long Beach or New York, gambling and drinking. Or you were at home, sleeping till three or four in the afternoon and then spending your evenings drinking to excess with your hometown buddies at the Russian Club, a membership bar walking distance from your mother's house. Sometimes you didn't make it all the way home and slept in the backyard garden until the sun woke you.

I treasured those visits to my grandmother's when you were home. On many occasions, I was seated at the kitchen table when you came down two flights of stairs from your third-floor bedroom to start your day in the late afternoon. You liked a breakfast of French toast sans butter and syrup; instead, you seasoned it with heavy doses of salt and pepper.

I watched you intently as you smoked unfiltered Camel cigarettes in rapid, uninterrupted succession, consuming them quickly with long, deep drags. You studied a horse racing book that had the weight and dimensions of the unabridged Oxford English Dictionary. You described the book as your bible. Your voice cracked the greasy air like gunshots, proclaiming your knowledge of horses, jockeys, and racetracks. You were driven to combine those three elements into winning bets. I couldn't look away from your ruddy face, drawn to your seemingly permanent squint, and fascinated by your detachment from the rules everyone else seemed to be playing by. Your lifestyle was clearly different from others, though I was too young to explain it or have more than a sketchy understanding of it. You had a sense of freedom in the manner in which you spoke, and at the same time, you made references to vague entities that you were determined never to let entrap you. I was too young to really understand what you talked about, but I got the impression that you were in a battle against forces that you warned would also endanger me.

You spoke poetically and mystically about standing your watch as the ship's lookout. You bore the responsibility of that job with military discipline, knowing that everyone's life depended upon your powers of concentration during those long, lonely hours. But you also conveyed a sense of wonder about the vastness of the ocean and the deep darkness that made your ship seem small and insignificant.

Aboard the ship, you lived like a priest, adhering to an enforced ascetic life. No drinking, no gambling, and no way to spend money. Off the ship, you thoroughly enjoyed unleashing all of your stored desires without restrictions.

Years later when my parents and I were living in California and I was in high school, you started to call us late in the evening about once a year, usually from a pay phone in a bar or on a street corner, just before you were preparing to board a ship for yet another across-the-world journey. You were always drunk and trying to make up for lost time in the hurried, boisterous minutes of the phone calls.

I always got my turn to speak with you, and I was treated to your pronouncements about geopolitics and conspiracy theories involving corrupt politicians. You said you knew what the federal government was up to, and you had recommendations about what I needed to do in order to avoid persecution. You assured me that one day we would have more time to talk, and you would spell things out for me so I could protect myself from evil forces.

You spoke like a member of the CIA or the Mafia, warning me that you couldn't divulge too much for fear of reprisals. "Someone is always listening," you said. I was entertained and enchanted. I wanted to believe that you really were "connected," and that you weren't just spouting nonsense fueled by alcohol. I wanted to be with you in the dive bar in San Francisco's Tenderloin District or one of your other points of departure, often New York City, ready to board a ship and escape the drudgery of high school and suburban life.

On one memorable occasion, you phoned us from Long Beach, California. You were not surprisingly in a bar, a few hours away from boarding a ship. We jumped in the car to see you, thinking we might never have another chance. The bar was in a seedy part of town, and only my father and I went in. My mother and sister remained in the car, with the doors locked.

You stood at a badly worn and scarred bar. You had a shot glass and beer in front of you. You were clearly feeling no pain as you engaged in a loud conversation with several other hardcore drinkers.

My father and I had to steady your legs as we pulled you out to the street so you could spend a few minutes with my mother and sister. The sunlight blinded you and you tried to pull all of us back into the bar. We stood our ground, trying to orchestrate some reasonable communion among family. You had a different agenda. You were too inebriated, incapable of showing any shred of coherence, affection, or sensitivity. You launched into an attack on my mother and sister. You called them "rich bitches." You said they were living a privileged life in California while my grandmother was back in Pennsylvania, suffering in impoverishment. My mother fought back tears as she took as much of your drunken ravings as she could stand. My father and I ushered you back into the bar and restored your place among your buddies, where you resumed a boisterous conversation without missing a beat. You were sucked immediately back into your whiskey and beer. No goodbye. No thanks for coming to meet me. No see you later.

Whenever you would call, my mother girded herself against your personal attacks. You would incoherently raise ancient family history and manufactured grievances, and never fail to accuse my mother of abandoning her mother and sister. My mother grew used to being assaulted by your phrase, "rich bitches." You were like a comedian who always told the same joke. There was no point in trying to rebut your accusatory tirades; we categorized them as the irrational ranting of an alcoholic.

When my mother could wedge a few words into your monologues, she tried to find out if you were physically okay, if you were taking care of yourself, and learn whatever details she could about your life aboard and between ships. You were miserly with personal information. "When I get on a ship, the first thing I do is make friends with the cook. Once I do that, everything is good. When I'm not on a ship, I'm at the track. I get home when I can."

Any longing I ever had in my fanciful fits of wanderlust to accompany you on board a ship or to a racetrack was destroyed by the meanness you displayed toward my mother and sister. I wondered if you reserved your heartless and spiteful tirades for family or if you treated everyone in the same manner.

As far as we knew, you didn't have a driver's license, a wife, or children. You never married, although you claimed to have ties to women in Hong Kong and Vietnam.

Toward the end of your life, I visited you with my father and Uncle Bob as companions. You had moved into your mother's house full time, your years of voyaging across the seas finally finished. Your mother was dead, and you were sitting in her faded yellow recliner, looking exactly like her in profile. I was shocked to see how your countenance had morphed into hers. Your wiry lean frame had been supplanted by surprising girth. Your ruddy complexion was now blistered deep red, the broken blood vessels much more prominent than I remembered from my youth, with sagging, plump jowls added to the mix.

The room was littered with copies of the local newspaper. You had twelve dirty soup bowls, precariously stacked on a tea tray. You never turned your eyes from the TV set to make eye contact with us. We tried to have a conversation with you, knowing that we would never see you again. It was late afternoon, and it didn't seem to us that you were in any physical condition to make your nightly visit to the Russian Club.

As I sat there in that dilapidated home, seeing my grandmother and then you occupying the same seat in a kind kaleidoscopic time warp, I had an urge to walk upstairs to see if your rifle was still leaning upright in the corner of your bedroom. But I really didn't need to; I'm certain it was still there. Where else would it be?

I sometimes wish my mother had been with us when we visited you. Then again, it's better that she was spared from seeing with her own eyes the sad figure you had become. She really didn't need proof.

Although I despised you for assaulting my mother and sister with your baseless, nasty incriminations, I'm still thankful for the intrigue and mystery you brought into my childhood.

PART FOUR: SONS

CHAPTER 19:
Never Too Late for a Happy Childhood

DEAR TRENT,

Through you, I have been able to discover the truth in the maxim, "It is never too late to discover a happy childhood." As your stepfather, I witnessed your happy childhood and thereby created one for myself. That is not to say that my childhood was all that bad. It wasn't. But yours was so much better, and for that, I'm proud of whatever small credit I may take for that, and I'm grateful that I was able to enjoy yours vicariously and thus re-live mine with greater appreciation that can only come from the perspective of age.

In the end, the small things are the most memorable and meaningful. Though that is an embarrassingly unoriginal thought, it possesses a timelessness and universality that is constantly reaffirmed for me.

Moments and days that we have shared stand out like the bumps on a relief map of my life. In my mind, I run my fingers over those raised areas over and over again, deepening my joy each time.

When you were about four years old, we were playing catch on the small patio of our condo. I could see the hard effort you were putting into developing your manual dexterity and hand-eye coordination. With each catch and throw, you were improving. At one point, you called a halt to our play and set the ball down with careful deliberation. In a voice resonating with independence and decisiveness, you said, "Michael, wait right here. This gum is spicy." You emphasized the word *spicy* like a professional broadcaster. You then went into the condo, spit out your gum, and returned to resume our play. Before picking up the ball, you checked to make sure that I had remained exactly where you had left me. You gave me a look that said, "Life can be unpleasant, but we can do something about it." This simple moment exemplified so much. You were taking charge of your own needs. You were exerting your will to affect another person's actions. You were announcing your displeasure at something that was offensive to your senses. You were displaying an interest in continuing to develop your dexterity and coordination, but on your own terms. Afterwards, your mother and I used your line, "This gum is spicy," whenever we reached a point in daily life when we wanted to call a halt to something and move in a different manner or direction. Repeating your words always made us remember the innocent, catalytic moment and laugh.

Some of my fondest memories of your childhood revolve around your school and day care experiences. Your mother and I used to refer to you as "Our little factory worker." This label stemmed from the long hours you spent on an elementary school campus. Our jobs entailed long commutes in opposite directions, requiring us to drop you off at daycare between 6:15 and 6:30 AM. You conducted yourself like a trooper, never complaining about the early start to your day. We weren't able to pick you up until 4:30 or 5 PM. There were occasions when we didn't get you until closer to 6, when daycare closed. Again, you never complained. In fact, there were days when you said we were picking you up too early. You had matured into a helper to the ladies who oversaw the school's day care facility. You helped prepare pancake breakfasts on Fridays, you escorted younger male students to the bathrooms, you ran errands to the office and other classrooms, and you helped put away toys, games, balls, and art supplies toward the end of the day. Your mother and I used to joke that you were an official part of the day care staff. Watching you take on such responsibility was incredibly joyful and made us exceedingly proud. There were days when I showed up at 5 to get you, and you looked at me with disappointment in your third-grader eyes. Then you would walk over to me and quietly say, "Give me fifteen minutes. I'm busy with something." I would laugh to myself, go for a walk around the campus, and give you the time you asked for, astounded that after being at school for about eleven hours, you still needed more time to complete your school day to your satisfaction.

A few years later, you revived for me the sweet angst and emotional disruption of a youthful, innocent romantic crush. You were playing Little League baseball and your mother and I inferred from the attention you were paying to a female first baseman on another team that you had a crush on her. I think you were in fifth grade. You asked if we could go to her game, which was scheduled a few hours before yours on a warm but breezy Tehachapi summer Saturday. Your mother and I shared a knowing wink and we said in unison, "Of course." At the ball field, we set up our folding chairs between first base and right field, getting you close but not too close to the object of your infatuation. It was fun to watch you squirm a little and object that our positioning was too obvious. We moved farther into right field. I don't remember your game, but I recall her game and watching you watch her. Your crush brought to mind one or two of my ancient youthful crushes, and I'm grateful to you for that.

Some time later, you convinced your mother and me to take you on a vehicle cruise by the girl's house, which was not far from where we lived. Your classmate lived on a cul-de-sac. The three of us piled into the front seat of my GMC Sierra and we set out for an innocent drive-by. Lo and behold, as I made the turn onto her street, we saw the girl and her father in their front yard. You and your mother quickly dove down to the floorboards of my truck and began laughing crazily. I was left exposed as I drove by their house and then had to negotiate a conspicuous U-turn in their cul-de-sac. It was summer, we had the windows down, and I felt quite naked. You and your mother saw the girl and her father before I did, and you two hit the floorboards instead of warning me not to make the turn. I couldn't get too upset; it was a funny moment that I wouldn't have missed for the world. You and your mother crouching down and out of sight was too precious a scene to miss out on. Seeing the two of you in a conspiratorial shenanigan, simultaneously erupting in laughter and trying weakly to subvert your outbursts, forms a perfect, priceless memory for me to forever cherish.

Trips to Knott's Berry Farm became our traditional way to mark the end of school and beginning of summer vacation. We started going when you were young enough to be enchanted by Camp Snoopy. Holding your hand as you frolicked through the park enabled me to relive my own experiences as a child going to an amusement park called Kennywood, near Pittsburgh, Pennsylvania. You gave me an opportunity to rediscover the untethered joy of riding roller coasters, eating cotton candy and funnel cakes, and wearing glow stick bracelets and necklaces. On one of our visits to Knott's Berry Farm, with your arm in a cast as a result of falling off a bike, you became the center of attention for younger kids at the hotel pool as you swam while holding your fluorescent green cast safely above the water line. You kept your arm dry from the pool, but it became saturated by the younger kids' fascination with your injury. I delighted in the constant attention you garnered. You were like a rock star fending off groupies.

When you were in junior high, you developed an interest in soccer, so much so that you worked for our local recreation center as a soccer referee for a youth league. Your mother and I delighted in watching you struggle to impose some sense of order and decorum among five- and six-year-olds who were trapped in chaos and pandemonium brought on naturally by their youth, ignorance, ineptitude, and inexperience. You also had to contend with parents who acted like they were watching World Cup matches. Your mother and I felt you were maturing at light speed between the games' beginning and ending whistles, having to calm enraged parents while instilling a sense of order in the games.

As a result of watching you grow and mature, my life has been enormously enriched and infused with delirious joy. Thank you for letting me be a part of your life. Through you I have lived my younger years twice, and the second time has been infinitely better.

DEAR JOHN-MICHAEL,

Safe to say that I was a far cry from the stepfather you would have chosen, and for me, you were a fair distance from an easy adjustment. Through your teenage years, we struggled mightily to find a way to coexist. We both paid a steep price for the effort, and I imagine the healing will continue for a while longer.

I'm proud that we never gave up. I'm proud that we backed away from truly tragic decisions. I'm proud that we refused to compromise our principles when doing so would have set us on a smoother course.

For two people who were at such pointed odds with each other for so many years, we are remarkably alike. We are both strong willed and stubborn. We refuse to give in. We insist that our steps are justified. We both are touched deeply by great literature, music, and film. We both have a fascination with Japanese culture. I taught English in Japan in the early '80s, eight years before you were born, and forty years later, you are teaching English in Japan. We both possess an independent, loner streak that tends to dominate our daily lifestyle. We have both battled personal demons and are mystified by people who seem to move through life with cavalier nonchalance.

Your youthful rebellion allowed me to revisit my own, and I wish I had shared with you how I saw myself in you and therefore understood what you were experiencing. Instead, I committed the same mistakes that my father committed when I was growing up. I met your insurgence with far too much resistance, judgment, and force. I foolishly tried to speed up your process of maturation and failed to give you the space you needed to develop at your own pace. I deeply regret my mistakes, and I'm proud of the way you endured them.

I hope you know that you have been blessed with a remarkably vibrant intelligence and capacity for creativity. Witnessing the manner in which you taught yourself to play guitar has been a delightful treat. Observing your talent to take hauntingly beautiful photographs serves as powerful evidence of your sensitive nature, your ability to see the world in a unique and poignant way, and your desire to express a profoundly insightful perspective on your surroundings. You also possess deep reservoirs of artistic and literary endowment, and your knowledge of music is extraordinary. You have so many options going forward of how to explore and display your abilities.

I'm proud of the way you persevered through school when it seemed disconnected from the things you cared about the most. I'm proud of the way you have fought to find a place in the world where you can exhibit your creativity and compassion. I'm proud of the place we have come to in our relationship, able now to express concern for each other, share, laugh, and look to a brighter future.

Thank you for not giving up on me. I hope you know that I will never give up on you.

PART FIVE:
INSPIRATION

DEAR ROBERTO CLEMENTE,

I got as close to you as I could but never close enough. I was given my first chance to see you when I was only five or six years old. My father used to take me to Pittsburgh Pirate games at Forbes Field after I had fallen in love with the game of baseball and I was learning from my father how to throw and catch. I had my own glove, an Ed Brinkman infield model, that was too big for my hand, but I still wore it like it was an organic part of me.

My love of baseball was part of my inheritance from my father. He coached US and Korean soldiers in Korea after the war ended and then coached me in my formative years. We spent hours in our backyard playing catch. He threw me grounders, flies, curve balls, knuckle balls, and all sorts of hard throws that required me to move laterally. He insisted on my using two hands, staying in front of the ball, and working on transitioning the ball from glove to hand for a quick return throw. It wasn't long before he had to put a sponge in his glove to handle the sting of my hardest throws.

My father used the *Pittsburgh-Post Gazette* to teach me to read. Reading the sports pages was my reward after he quizzed me on the front page as well as national and international sections. Articles about Pirates' games invariably included details about Clemente's batting, fielding, and base running exploits. I read about him with my father's help before I ever laid eyes on him. Then I saw him on TV, making basket catches in right field and pegging runners from the outfield warning track all the way to third base, his rocket arm making the ball fly "on a rope," cutting the air like a missile.

Inside Forbes Field, hours before the game, my father and I stood behind the batting cage, intently watching Clemente take batting practice and play catch with a teammate. Approaching the batting cage, he moved his neck and twisted his back as if he was too stiff to swing the bat. He moved his head like a bird, poking and thrusting and tilting it in all directions. He looked like he was trying to overcome an injury. Then he would step into the cage and ferociously unleash a powerful swing that erased any suspicion of injury or disability. His batting stance appeared too nonchalant. His feet seemed to be planted too deep and away in the batter's box. Then his wrists and arms exploded in a burst of movement, and when his bat struck the ball, it sounded like gunfire. When he paired off with a teammate for warm-up throws, his very first toss was hard and straight. He didn't seem to need to warm up.

I would beg my father to buy tickets in the right field bleachers, so we could be close to Clemente. He usually relented, but sometimes he wanted to sit behind home plate so I could appreciate the velocity of the pitchers and see the balls and strikes along with the umpire. It was also an opportunity to see Clemente at bat closely, to appreciate his raw strength and explosive bat and base running speed. I was enthralled by his mere presence in the on-deck circle. He usually bent down on one knee and took a few practice swings from his kneeling position. His wrists seemed ready to uncoil with lethal power.

No matter where we sat, I was in awe, as was my father. We were enchanted by his famous signature basket catches, and we delighted in his throws from deep right field to prevent runners from advancing or scoring. I was inspired by Clemente to develop my baseball skills and also to apply myself to other endeavors, both intellectual and physical, with his brand of devotion and enthusiasm.

Clemente represented for me the elegance of sport, the poetry of athleticism, and the selflessness of loyalty to one team and one city. I loved Clemente before I knew of his Puerto Rican heritage, his importance as a pioneer in the matriculation of Latin ballplayers into the major leagues, and the quiet humble example he set for gracefully overcoming hardship, prejudice, oppression, and all manner of obstacles. He became such a pioneering representative not just of Latin and Black athletes, but of all people who are stereotyped, oppressed, and mistreated based on skin color, accents, and heritage. With grace and humanity, Clemente transcended sports and will live forever as an endearing champion of human dignity. No other sports figure has ever captured my veneration and devotion in the manner of Clemente. No other ever will.

When he died in a plane crash while attempting to deliver food and supplies to the victims of the devastating Nicaraguan earthquake in 1972, I cried openly with my father, accompanied him to church to pray for Clemente's soul, and lit votive candles for his family. Forever afterwards, the game of professional baseball was diminished for both of us by Roberto Clemente's absence. Until my father's death in 2010, he found no one in professional sports worthy of the adulation and admiration he had for Clemente. I stopped looking for a suitable replacement in professional sports for my adulation and admiration for Clemente long ago.

DEAR DODGER,

Thank you for more than living up to your reputation as "man's best friend." You unleashed upon me a decade of joy, loyalty, love, empathy, enthusiasm, and understanding. I pray that there is an afterlife for beautiful creatures like you, and I pray that I will be fortunate enough to see you again in another realm. I want to feel the urgency of your shepherd/chow paws upon my chest and the anticipation of your muzzle against my neck.

I miss the way that you instinctively enriched our walks, teaching me to pause and reflect rather than simply complete the steps in robotic, insentient fashion, as I otherwise would have done. I miss the way that you woke when I woke, slept when I slept, walked when I walked, ran when I ran, stretched out on the floor when I stretched out on the floor, pressing your back against mine or draping your forearm across my chest. I can still feel the touch of your pure, loving, irreplaceable gestures.

I miss the way you leaped into the rear seat of my truck, your face taking up the whole area of my rearview mirror, the way you waited patiently for me to secure your leash, the way you reminded me of my underappreciated sense of smell, the way you balanced caution with curiosity as we approached a herd of deer or elk.

You were such an alpha male, unable to coexist with your brother, displaying fierce fighting ability at feeding times, willing to sustain injury to stand your ground. We kept you because you were nursing a deep wound on your nose from a brotherly encounter, and we found a suitable home for Angel. You seemed to be in a permanent state of bliss to have the house to yourself and to lose a rival, even one of blood. You were too happy and content to ever be lonely, much to our surprise.

I'm sorry for the deep gash you sustained jumping over our chain link fence. You were such an explorer and just couldn't resist. The wire fence was a mistake, and you were much happier and better protected when we replaced it with ranch-style fence posts and chicken wire. I'll always remember the way you tried to keep your wound from us, no doubt wanting to save us from guilt. You endured the trip to the vet with great stoicism, along with the stitches and recovery. Whenever I gently touched the scar on the inside of your groin, you looked at me with guilt in your eyes, absolving me of any responsibility.

Thank you for letting me hug, kiss, hold, pet, and massage you. Thank you for putting up with all of my moods.

Near the end, when you could no longer drink, eat, or leap into the rear seat of my truck, I know that you knew what needed to be done. The cancer diagnosis was mere confirmation of knowledge we already possessed. I am forever heartbroken at having to empty your bowls full of water and food, and to lift you in and out of my truck. But I am equally forever blessed to have had ten years of loving companionship with you, and I am still in awe of your courage as we lay on the vet's floor together, and you allowed me to hold you as he administered the shot that relieved all of your pain. I am still beside you, holding you, wherever you are now.

DEAR TEACHERS AND PROFESSORS OF LITERATURE,

Stories have picked me up from moribund inertia and transported me to destinations that were beyond my imagination and desire. Stories have awakened in me thoughts and feelings that were embryonic or dormant. Stories have ignited my senses, enabling me to comprehend divergent viewpoints and lifestyles that I otherwise would have ignored or judged harshly and unfairly. Stories have delivered me to settings that otherwise would have remained distant and unknown. Stories have exploded the concept of chronological time, deepening the dimensions of my experience to fathoms otherwise beyond my reach.

I am forever indebted to the teachers and professors who have taught me how to comprehend the deepest layers and implications of an author's words, how to analyze a character's motives and actions, how to uncover insights into the human condition, how to evaluate behavior patterns and measure intended and unintended consequences, and how not to merely recognize beauty but to analyze its subtle nuances and infinite permutations.

Being able to lose myself in a piece of literature has been a profound and invaluable way for me to find myself. Literature has given me depictions of reality that make actual reality more discernible. Literature has given me examples of idealism that have inspired me to seek idealism in my own life and in the world. Literature has given me fantasy that has made the real world easier to accept and endure.

Thank you for acting as my Sherpa up the mountains of Plato, Aristotle, Sophocles, Shakespeare, Milton, Dickinson, Whitman, and Twain. Thank you for helping me to set up camp in the worlds of Hemingway, Fitzgerald, Faulkner, O'Neill, Williams (Tennessee and William Carlos), Wilder, Miller, Lee, and Hansberry.

I sat mesmerized in your classrooms as you made sense of the word and thus of the world, excavating nuggets of golden epiphanies in dense passages of text. You guided me through the process of ascertaining, analyzing, and interpreting the ideals of human achievement and the depths of human depravity. You armed me with your expert skills of explication, which have served me so well outside of the classroom and in all manner of private and public settings. By learning how to read text, I have learned how to read people and read life. I have learned that "the red wheelbarrow" is not simply and strictly a wheelbarrow. I have learned how to tell my own story with more accuracy, precision, and effect. And that, as William Carlos Williams wrote, "has made all the difference."

CHAPTER 24:
Second Chances

DEAR VANESSA,

Thank you for helping a wounded and grieving soul heal. Thank you for crawling down into my personal abyss and helping me crawl out. Thank you for believing in someone who had stopped believing in himself. Thank you for accepting my many limitations and faults and encouraging me to reconcile them, helping me to push them out of my path of progress, and urging me to concentrate on my strengths and aspirations. Thank you for giving me space to remember and honor my past, and for encouraging me to look to the future with more optimism than regret. Thank you for reminding me that giving and receiving love is the most important thing.

Thank you for embarking with me on a second chance, knowing that the past casts long shadows, but being willing to work together to make sure those shadows don't block tomorrow's sun.

Thank you for risking everything, knowing that second chances may go the way of first chances.

You have shared with me your most vulnerable self, and I have tried my best to be protective. You have shown me your most indestructible self, and I have tried my best to strengthen it more. You have been equally protective of me, and you have strengthened me in ways that I could not strengthen myself.

Thank you for giving me space and time to figure out the next stage of my life, with winter bearing down and fewer options on the table. You have helped me see that having fewer options enhances the meaning and quality of those that remain.

Thank you for pushing me to engage in the process of healing myself, knowing that it would not occur naturally without concrete steps and strategies.

Thank you for adjusting to and accepting a different frame of reference. I'm sure I have made you want to leap from my truck when I refused to tune my Sirius channel to anything other than Springsteen or Petty.

Thank you for spending time with all my dead heroes of film: Bogart, Gable, Stewart, Wayne, Tracy, Sinatra, Newman, and Scott.

Thank you for tolerating the verbosity of an incessant and irrecoverable English teacher. Your patience has never broken. You have forsaken so many straight lines to follow me as I meander and wander.

Thank you for that peaceful interlude on a hotel balcony overlooking the Pacific when so much was at stake and so much was possible. You made the sun feel different; you made me want to see it again, to believe in the promise of tomorrow.

Thank you for your part in building a bridge between different cultures, languages, and upbringings. We have both discovered that what lies on either side of the bridge is far more alike than different.

Thank you for affirming the glory of family despite all its foibles, faults, and fissures.

Thank you for not allowing my cynicism to corrupt your faith.

I have been awed by your capacity to overcome unbearable

violation and exploitation in so many respects, without losing your beautiful heart that remains full of forgiveness, tenderness, and love.

Thank you for being my "Brown Eyed Girl."

PART SIX: JAPAN

DEAR SHIRO YAMAGUCHI,

I am older now than you were when you died. I can still feel the sting of your relatively early death, and my longevity is diminished by your absence. I knew you for such a short time, but your impact on me was profound, more so now that I am so much older and you are gone.

We met in the early 1980s when I was teaching English in Japan. You came to me as a Japanese businessman who wanted to enlarge his English vocabulary, improve his conversational fluency, and broaden his understanding of idioms. You wanted to be able to use English to explore and express ideas in more depth.

Initially, you said that you worked for a Japanese stationery company and the ability to converse competently in English was necessary in your sales position. Soon I realized that your real motivation was to engage in intellectual tête-à-têtes using English rather than your native tongue. I quickly learned that you possessed a brilliant mind and needed a new challenge in your fifth decade.

I was working for a private English conversation school in Osaka, your hometown, and that is how our paths crossed. Then, I was in my mid-twenties, and you were a few years past the half-century mark.

You always came into our forty-five-minute sessions dressed professionally in a suit and tie. You always wore your thinning hair slicked back with precision, and your suits barely contained a rugged, muscular frame. Later, I learned that as a youth you played rugby, and you still played on an aging team that was as competitive now as it had been some forty years earlier. You were dismissive in a light-hearted way of American football with its pads and helmets. You considered your thick, steely muscles protection enough against the brutal hits and tackles.

At first, we met at the English-language school that employed me. You were uncomfortable in tiny meeting rooms where we bumped knees and endeavored to block out English lessons going on in other tiny rooms. The school consisted of six or seven such rooms, closets, really, cut out in odd angles in a claustrophobia-inducing office space on the first floor of an apartment building in an industrial part of the city. After a few such meetings, we began to rendezvous for our lessons at a coffee shop owned by your sister. My school facilitated these "away" lessons. I usually arrived first, and your sister always served me a piping hot, deliciously strong cup of coffee. She never permitted me to pay.

When you arrived, she would bring you coffee and offer me a second cup. In Japan, coffee was made to order and sold by the individual cup, and I couldn't resist saying yes to her offer, despite my guilt that I was drinking for free. I don't know if your sister simply "comped" me or if you took care of the charges. You politely dismissed my attempts to pay or reimburse you later.

If I didn't have a lesson scheduled after yours, at another location, we would sit and talk far beyond our forty-five-minute class. You often invited me to sushi shops, tempura eateries, or bars to continue our conversation. Your appetite for English vocabulary was insatiable, and I needed little convincing to learn how to eat squid, octopus, and abalone, among other tempting Japanese delicacies. You taught me how to enjoy Japanese beer, sake, and Suntory whiskey all at the same time. Combining all of these types of alcohol in one sitting ran against my better judgment, but I willingly consented to your customs. You enjoyed my reticence, and I enjoyed your persuasion.

To call myself a teacher when I met you is at best a misnomer and at worst fraudulent. I was a native English speaker, and that was the only qualification required of me. Despite my youth, inexperience, and naïveté, you and your sister bestowed upon me the title of sensei. (In today's political and cultural climate, I would probably be accused by some of White and linguistic privilege.) You and your lovely sister held no such prejudice.

As I reflect all these years later upon our conversations, we seemed to be playing a kind of verbal chess. The purpose of the game was not to win; rather, it was to improve each other's skill in articulating our ideas with precision, depth, nuance, and respect. You were so profoundly sincere, so determined to enrich your English skills, so intent on understanding America and helping me understand Japan.

Working as a salesman for a Japanese stationery company, you sold products all over the world; hence, your need for transactional English conversation skills was authentic. But this need paled in comparison to your hunger to engage in deep conversations about a wide range of substantive topics: literature, philosophy, government, culture, entertainment, and sports.

You revered me as if I were an ambassador of America. You conducted yourself with such meticulousness of thought, as if you were an ambassador of Japan, though you would have humbly deflected such a description. Within a few lessons, our English conversations evolved into a kind of cultural diplomacy, anchored by linguistic learning, without arrogance, pretension, or self-interest. You concentrated and spoke as if you were moving chess pieces on the board, with care, delicacy, and exactitude.

During one lesson, you introduced me to the Nobel Laureate Yasunari Kawabata who, like yourself, was a native son of Osaka. You gave me a copy of his lyrical masterpiece, *Snow Country*, and I read it before our next session, like a student meeting a teacher's deadline. Kawabata's spare but luminous prose brought to mind the poets William Carlos Williams and Emily Dickinson, and we spent hours analyzing the works of these and other literary giants.

In our conversations, you asked me to explain American culture and politics. You had so many questions that I needed to do research before our lessons and arrive with texts, which you consumed with great passion and energy. At times, I felt we were graduate students preparing for our oral exams.

Even as we developed a close, intense friendship and began to socialize, you insisted on continuing our formal lessons. I continued to drink your sister's delectable coffee. We spent countless hours eating sushi and tempura and drinking. We walked the streets of Osaka in the blistering heat of summer, the blustery cold of winter, and in the relentlessly wet monsoon season. During monsoon season, we ran in unison through the city streets for the protection of train platforms and subway stations.

When we overindulged, we sought out your favorite Chinese eatery, an open-air walk-up that was nothing more than a red Formica counter barely long enough for five seats in an out-of-the-way location in the city center, a hidden gem that a foreigner like me would never find on his own. There, we steadied our weaving bodies by eating delicious gyoza and sharing large bottles of Kirin beer.

There are words you spoke to me nearly forty years ago that have stayed with me, indelible as if you had carved them in stone. You described what it was like as a young boy to hear the rumbling American B-29 bombers as they flew over Osaka, fearing that a strike in your vicinity would incinerate your cheaply constructed wooden house and instantly wipe away your family. The American planes flew low enough for you not only to hear but also to see from your hiding place, which was nothing more than a closet. You said the menacing sound of the American planes had never left you. You heard it in your sleep, you heard it in your daydreams, you heard it when you were shaving, you heard it when you were standing on a train platform, and you heard it when you were sitting next to your wife at night drinking tea and watching television.

We contemplated the many and sundry forms of evil that consumed individuals and worlds with a perverse form of immortality.

You apologized directly and passionately to me for Japan's mistakes in following the malevolent Emperor Hirohito, in aligning itself with Hitler's Germany, in declaring war against America through the attack on Pearl Harbor, and in betraying the Japanese people by embarking on an immoral quest for power. In doing so, you taught me about love of country, about nationalism in the best sense of that word, about humility, about grace, about forgiveness, about individual connection to country, about individual and collective responsibility. You taught me that loving one's country is an honorable act. You taught me that it's possible for an individual to embody the best qualities of his or her country, and to live his life in a way that brings honor to his country. You taught me that a sense of place could be given an animate life force and made to flourish inside a person.

I want most of all for these words to be my conveyance of thanks for being my teacher so much more than I ever was your teacher. I miss your friendship so deeply. I miss eating sushi with you, always squid and tuna first. I miss drinking with you. I miss walking all over Osaka with you, feeling such a welcomed part of that marvelous city's energy and vibrancy. I miss visiting Japanese temples and shrines with you, minimizing my breathing and movement, and listening to the silence that can only be expressed by deity. I miss learning about Japanese baseball players and Sumo wrestlers and watching you watch their performances with such pride and devotion. I miss discussing matters of silliness and substance with you. I miss standing on a train platform late at night, enjoying a break from relentless rain, shivering, searching for the right words, waiting for our trains. I miss your wave of your hand, after a handshake, part salute, part prayer for safe travels and continuing friendship.

You helped me look inside myself to make discoveries that I otherwise wouldn't have made. You helped me transcend myself to make discoveries about the world that I otherwise would have missed.

After I left Japan, I heard from a friend that you had died of stomach cancer. I hope that I was able to express my deep and everlasting gratitude to you when I knew you. If not, these words are my feeble attempt to do so now, hoping that somehow you are aware of how I will always feel about you. To my sensei, Godspeed.

DEAR UNKNOWN JAPANESE BUSINESSMEN,

Sometimes the kindness of strangers is required to rescue a person from his own naïveté and ignorance. In my early twenties, I found myself in a situation that I was completely unprepared for. Were it not for strangers who recognized my vulnerability and who enveloped me in their benevolence, my course of action might have been much different.

I was teaching English in Osaka, Japan's second great megalopolis, and I had to leave the country for a few days in order to renew my work visa. The private school I was working for made arrangements for me to travel to Seoul, South Korea. The school booked my flights and hotel accommodations; all I had to do was get to the airport and locate my Japanese liaison/translator who would guide me through my excursion. Simple enough.

I had only been in Japan for six months and I was still discovering nuances of Japanese culture. My quick three-day trip to Seoul revealed quite a few cultural gradations that represented an "adult portion," to borrow the esteemed Levon Helm's phrase in describing the Band's first trip to New York City. My inexperience and unfamiliarity were on full display, and I definitely needed to be rescued.

I recall vividly the pleasant taxi ride to the airport. Public transportation in Japan was marvelously efficient and indulging. Japanese taxi drivers dressed in the utmost professional attire: white gloves, crisply ironed shirts, ties, vests, and slacks. Their taxis were maintained in pristine condition inside and out. White, creaseless covers were stretched snugly over the seats. Floors were kept free of dirt and trash. Windows were carefully polished. Spotless doilies decorated the headrests.

Taxi drivers who lined up outside train and subway stations, shopping districts, and hotels routinely exited their cabs while they waited for fares, to shine windows, headlamps, and bumpers, even in winter. Drivers clearly prided themselves on the cleanliness of their cabs.

My trip happened to be in winter, and the cab was delightfully warm. Drivers were consistently friendly, patient, calm, methodical, and tolerant of dizzying traffic congestion, putting passengers at ease by displaying expert driving skills. Drivers regularly emphasized their turns and lane changes with polite hand gestures, flat palms cutting the space in front of the steering wheel, as if they were communicating with other drivers and punctuating their concentration on Japan's extraordinarily narrow and congested roads.

At the airport, I quickly found my point of contact with my name on a signboard, as if I were taking part in a formal tour. The guide also had a colorful flag raised high above her head as a calling symbol. I soon realized that I would be traveling with a group of Japanese businessmen as they were gathering alongside me. We handed over our passports and luggage and took our seats to wait for the boarding call. As I sat in the airport, I contemplated my inclusion in a travel group. My employers had said nothing to me about this arrangement, but I felt confident that everything had been taken care of and that I had nothing to worry about.

The experience of flying on Korean Airlines was far superior to any American airline I had ever flown on, and equal to my experience on Japan Airlines with gracious flight attendants, spacious seating, warm hand towels, sensitive service, and a fresh, delicious meal. The only downside was the less than two hours flying time. I would have enjoyed the attentive service for a longer duration.

In Seoul, our guide informed my travel cluster of some twenty-five Japanese businessmen that our luggage would be transported to the hotel for us. We were then shuttled from the airport to our hotel in the city center, a trip of a little more than an hour. The guide checked all of us into our rooms and then asked us to convene in a few hours in the hotel lobby. I figured maybe we would all be going out to dinner or on a city sightseeing tour. Silly me.

After a walk through the city, I met my guide and travel companions in the hotel lobby. I stood listening to much conversation and started to wonder what all the anxious discussion was about. It seemed more involved than just dinner and sightseeing. Despite my ignorance of the Japanese language, I could tell that the guide was going through specific instructions. Among the businessmen, there was much chatter, many questions, laughter, and smiles. I knew something was afoot, as Sherlock Holmes would say, but I had no idea what it was.

A few of the businessmen observed my confusion and approached me. Their faces were marked by wry smiles. One of the gentlemen said in halting but clearly enunciated English, "I would be happy to translate for you." He proceeded to explain that the guide would soon be escorting everyone to a Korean house of prostitution. The businessmen would have an opportunity to select a female companion who would then be spending the entire night with them. Although I was the only non-Japanese in the group, the guide had obviously assumed that I would be going along with all the others. She had made the assumption that I had known from the outset that I was part of a Japanese sex tour. She knew nothing of my need to renew my work visa. The businessman seemed to enjoy explaining all of this to me. He and his companions watched my reaction intently and seemed to relish in my surprise. He didn't need me to say anything to figure out that I had no intention of "buying" a lady for the evening. He then engaged in a conversation with his three buddies who had encircled me. Their conversation was intense and animated. I stood awkwardly and waited.

I was internally fuming that my employers had arranged for me to be part of a sex tour. I wondered if they thought I would be thankful upon my return. I wondered how they could have so little regard for my right to know what they were getting me into, denying me a chance to agree or refuse to participate. Were the travel arrangements simply the most economical for them, as they were paying for my trip? Regardless of my employers' intentions, I felt very much like *The Ugly American* from the 1958 novel by William J. Lederer and Eugene Burdick that I had read in college.

After a few minutes, the spokesman turned to me and easily read my consternation. He placed a hand on my shoulder and told me everything would be all right. He then extended an invitation to join him and his friends in his hotel room to spend the evening playing cards and drinking Suntory whiskey. He and his buddies had decided to deviate from the evening's formal agenda.

I have often wondered if the gentleman and his friends felt sorry for me and decided to stay behind at the hotel to keep me company, or whether they had never intended to obtain a prostitute. I do know that I had a very enjoyable evening playing poker and drinking whiskey. The men explained to me that Japanese "sex tours" were commonplace. Not wanting to be impolite, I refrained from asking if they ever participated. I learned that all of the men were married, and that their wives understood their need to enjoy some male companionship on three-day getaways. I chose not to ask them to define the word "enjoy."

About an hour after the tour departed to pick up the prostitutes, some of the other businessmen came by our room to show off their dates. That part of the evening was quite uncomfortable and embarrassing. The prostitutes looked to be in their early twenties, some perhaps a bit younger. The middle-aged men displayed no self-consciousness, much less shame. They showed off the young women with pride and barely contained excitement.

Later on, during my stint teaching English in Japan, I learned how prevalent the appetite for prostitutes was among a segment of Japanese men. I learned to spot the garish "love hotels" in Osaka that rented rooms by the hour. I was introduced to hostess bars filled with young women from Korea and the Philippines who catered to the egos of men who indulged in having their cigarettes lit, their whiskey glasses filled and stirred, and their thighs and shoulders rubbed with teasing fealty. I learned that many Japanese men spent their workday evenings with mistresses and then would return home near midnight to a waiting, subservient wife who had hot tea and a meal at the ready.

While in Japan, I read about the nation's history of invasion, colonization, and subjugation of the Korean peninsula. I encountered firsthand the lasting bitterness between the two countries in my friendships and associations with both Korean and Japanese people. I met Koreans who, while living in Japan, kept their ancestry a secret for fear of being ostracized and discriminated against. I talked with Japanese people who referred to Korea as a culturally inferior country. I learned from Koreans that they felt many Japanese people took for granted that Korea was a geographical buffer between Japan and a threatening China.

After working in Japan for nearly a year, I discovered that the two brothers who owned and operated the private school where I taught were Korean, but they passed themselves off as Japanese. My Korean sex tour experience took on an ironic element that remains a mystery to me all these years later.

I'm grateful that four Japanese businessmen rescued me from an indelicate and morally corrupt occasion. I would like to think that under no circumstances would I have acquiesced to the proposition that was presented to me in that hotel lobby to secure a prostitute. But I was young, single, lonely, and sometimes impetuous, a ripe target for a foolish, wrong-headed decision. In any case, I'm deeply thankful and appreciative for those kind men coming to my aid and educating me when I was so blissfully naïve and ignorant.

CHAPTER 27:
Gaijin

DEAR PEOPLE OF JAPAN,

I owe you so much. You sometimes called me gaijin (foreigner), but you did so in an endearing, not insulting, way. You always treated me like a favored son.

You approached me on the street, on subways and trains, and in restaurants and bars, and asked if you could practice your English on me. You wanted to demonstrate your reverence for America by proving your understanding of English grammar. You simply needed a chance to converse. You wanted to test your knowledge of American history, cinema, music, and culture. You wanted to prove your credentials as a student of America.

You extended to me status that I deserved only in your eyes. You gave me the seat of honor at tables in your homes and restaurants. You served me before anyone else. You gave me the choicest bowls of soup with the fish head proud and prominent and most delectable cuts of fish and meat.

You conveyed your love of America and respect for me as an American in every conversation and encounter.

You welcomed me into your sushi and tempura shops and taught me your country's culture and history through food. You accepted me as one of your own by elbowing and pushing me on subway and train platforms as an affirmation of Darwin's "survival of the fittest" theory. Inside the subway and train cars, you allowed yourself to be pressed against my body along with your fellow countrymen and women, expecting me to do my part in filling every crevice of space as a condition of commuting in a small country with a large population.

You welcomed me into your disco clubs and played extra songs by Donna Summer, KC and the Sunshine Band, and the Bee Gees in recognition of the American on your dance floor. You exploded in raucous cheering when I sang "My Way" and "Love Me Tender" in your karaoke bars, and you never admitted that you sang those songs better than I did, without needing the words printed out, to celebrate and honor my presence.

In the center of your megacity of Osaka, with a population approaching twenty million, you let me sleep in summer with my apartment doors and windows wide open without having to fear an intruder. You let me walk safely and freely in all parts of your cities—industrial centers, shopping districts, restaurant and bar streets, suburban and rural areas at all hours of day and night—without ever once fearing for my safety.

You stopped me on the street to ask me questions about Elvis Presley, Marilyn Monroe, Henry Aaron, UCLA, Disneyland, Hollywood, the Grand Canyon, and so many other iconic symbols about America that you cherished and celebrated.

You apologized for WWII; you thanked me for America's commitment to reconstructing Japan after the war. At memorials and museums in Hiroshima and Nagasaki, you approached me and bowed, shook my hand, hugged me, prayed with me, and agreed that we had to remember our past in order to build a better future.

You taught me the value of hierarchy, national pride, shame, unity, solidarity, peace, tradition, humility, hard work, and ceremony. You taught me that one individual has the capacity to encompass the qualities that create a country. You taught me the value of a national identity that can be instilled in its citizens through family structure and formal education in order to strengthen the individual and the nation he or she represents. You taught me to be suspicious of cleverness. You taught me the beauty of silence.

PART SEVEN: LEARNING AND TEACHING

CHAPTER 28:
The Making of a Writer

DEAR DAVE,

I encountered you when I foolishly thought that I knew more than I actually did and when I thought I had skills as a writer that I wholly lacked. I was overly confident and naïve.

You quickly realized that my talent as a writer was latent and undisciplined, and you generously decided to do something about it.

You were the managing editor of a medium-size newspaper, and I was a lost but eager young man who was trying to find his way and willing to take a risk. Desperate to get my life going in America after two years of teaching English in Japan, I bolted into your newspaper and applied for a job as a reporter.

My move that day was impulsive and fueled by an overestimation of my knowledge and talents. All I knew was that your newspaper needed a reporter and I convinced you that I was willing to work in the middle of the night to gather police report data for a crime log and generate compelling stories that could be extracted from law enforcement arrests and activities and other first-responder calls.

Essentially, you had an unoccupied desk for a bottom-rung reporter, and I was able-bodied, bolstered with a degree in English and a record as a teacher, presumably meaning I could write cogent, grammatically correct sentences in English.

After putting me through a writing test, in which I was given a set of facts and asked to organize them into a three-paragraph story, I was hired, much to my surprise. Your grading of my story was more exact and brutal than any feedback I had ever received in sixteen years of formal education. In short, clipped statements, barely moving your lips and without eye contact, you pointed out the shortcomings of my writing. My sentences were reasonably fine for a fiction writer but not for a reporter, and there were too many of them. My organization of the facts was woefully inadequate. I took too long to get to the main point. I failed to collect key facts in as few sentences as possible. I demonstrated no respect for my reader, wasting his time by delaying the story's essence and making him sort through unnecessary details. Other than those objections, my test performance was lovely.

The newspaper's executive editor agreed with your decision to hire me, despite your bloody critique.

I was instructed to shadow another reporter the following morning to begin learning the job. I was shown a bare desk with a cumbersome computer terminal and push-button phone. The reporter I was going to shadow retrieved a chair from the corner of the newsroom where it had been abandoned for reasons I was soon to discover. One of its four wheels was jammed and nonfunctioning; consequently, the chair didn't roll as intended. The seat cushion was badly frayed, exposing yellow stuffing that felt scratchy like asbestos. The spring-loaded back support was stuck in a rigid, upright position. The desk drawers were barren: no pens, paper, paper clips, or notebooks. On one corner of the desk sat a stack of the recent editions of the paper. You told me to buy a reporter's notebook and read the cop logs to get an idea of what I would be writing.

I stationed myself at the sterile desk, and I tried to look like I belonged. Instead, I felt conspicuous. People were either bouncing around like pinballs through the maze of desks, or they had their faces glued to computer screens. The sound of fingers banging on keyboards caused a sense of panic that made it hard for me to breathe or sit still. I was used to writing my college papers in a quiet room, by myself. I didn't belong here. I couldn't type that fast; I couldn't think that fast. I couldn't cradle a phone against my neck, talk, jot down notes, and type, all at the same time. I didn't even know how to turn my computer terminal on.

People glanced at me as if I were an intruder with a communicable disease.

This was a fight-or-flight moment.

I turned to the first cop log and found it impossible to concentrate. I read the same sentence over and over without comprehension. Just when I thought I could move on to the next sentence, a phone would ring louder than a church bell and I would have to go back to the first sentence and start over. I was a fraud, an imposter.

I was hired as a writer and I was finding out that I couldn't even read, much less write, in this environment. My clothing began to strangle me. The chair felt like a straightjacket. I started to sweat like a criminal under interrogation.

I'm not sure how I resisted the urge to quit on the spot and hightail it out of an environment that I knew nothing about, and one that I was utterly unequipped to handle. I forced myself to stay seated in my rigid chair and go through all the cop logs in all the papers that were stacked up on my desk. I waited until Dave left for the day before I dared get up, use the restroom, and slink away.

I experienced a night of soul-searching. I had thrust myself into a foreign situation and I had to muster what my father had taught me during my formative years in order to work my way through it. He had always told me to have the "courage of my convictions," and

I had to prove to him that I learned that lesson.

Dave, you put me at ease the following morning. You accepted the reality that I was a neophyte in the newspaper business, and that I would be facing a steep learning curve. You promised to help me make the climb, as long as I was willing to put in the hours. You urged me not to pretend that I knew something when I didn't. "Ask me," you said.

You gave me time and space to learn, but you demanded proof that I was, in fact, making progress. The newspaper had inches of space to fill with copy, and it was my job as one of your reporters to fill up those columns of space with something worth printing.

Whenever I submitted an article that I had written poorly, you sent it back to me with specific instructions on how to rewrite it. Sometimes, when we were on a deadline, you rewrote my copy and sent it to the printer with my name on it. "You're the writer; I'm the editor. Every writer needs one."

You understood better than anyone what an undisciplined novice I truly was in the art and science of writing. I don't know why you took on the task of teaching me how to think, how to work under pressure, how to identify the important bits of information that readers would find compelling, how to interview a source to elicit information that would only emerge if the right questions were asked, and how to focus one's concentration on the task at hand and erase nonessential noise and input, like an elite athlete.

Your job was hard enough without nursemaiding me into a journalist.

From your bunker in the center of the newsroom, you taught me how to interact with law enforcement officers and city officials and walk away with kernels of information that other news outlets didn't have. You taught me how to transform scribbled notes at 4 AM about a capsized boat into a dramatic Coast Guard rescue that warranted a front-page, above-the-fold story, instead of a mere dry blurb in the police log.

You taught me how to cover a city council meeting from 7 till 11:30 PM, return to the dormant newsroom at midnight, and compose and file two front-page stories before 3 AM.

You taught me how to scour police and sheriff's logs at 4 AM, identify the incidents that could be expanded into front-page stories, return to the newsroom to make follow-up calls, produce fourteen inches of crime report entries with all the facts correct, and then write the expanded stories, all by the 8 AM deadline.

You taught me to write every word with readers in mind, respecting their time and satisfying their curiosity with accurate, interesting, and worthwhile information.

You helped me strengthen my writing with economy, discipline, and purpose.

I am deeply in your debt and offer an eternally grateful thanks for being a phenomenal editor and an even better teacher.

DEAR PHIL KRAFT,

As a new teacher trying to comprehend the mindset of recalcitrant students and searching desperately for ways to reach them, you met me in my moments of deepest despair. You gave me wise counsel and warm collegiality.

You were a veteran English teacher and you comforted me by pointing out that even the world's greatest teachers had students who were incorrigible, disobedient, and defiant. You reminded me that Jesus had his Judas, Aristotle had his Alexander, and Seneca had his Nero. Therefore, I should not be surprised to encounter in my classroom challenging students who might ultimately prove to remain, at least during the time that I knew them, beyond my influence.

Still, you insisted that I owed them my best intentions, care, knowledge, ability, and scholarship. You reassured me that I would eventually be successful with a majority of my students, and that I would have to accept that my impact might be delayed, unconfirmed by tangible evidence, or marked by failure with some students. But, in all cases, the effort was worth it, regardless of the results.

Thank you for putting things in perspective for me, as only you could. Thank you for listening to my self-doubt and for patiently and meticulously reassembling the pieces of my shattered confidence. Thank you for lifting my spirits when they were low. Thank you for restoring my belief that even as a confused, inexperienced teacher with so much more to learn, I still had something worthwhile to offer.

Thank you for filling up my classroom with hundreds of books, magazines, and assorted instructional materials when I had virtually nothing, sitting forlornly in a barren classroom a few days before school's opening and wondering where and how to begin creating a rich, vibrant learning environment.

You were so unassuming and tender, rolling carts of materials over to my room for two solid days, telling me that your classroom was overstuffed and you needed to de-clutter. Each time you entered my classroom pushing a cart loaded with materials, you said, "A few more things, you might find a use for them." Always, "A few more . . . a few more."

I had done nothing to deserve such concern except move into a classroom next door to yours as a first-year teacher without a clue. "A few more . . . a few more. Do what you want with these; toss them if you can't use them." You were so empathetic, so reassuring, and so prescient. "Everything will come together; you'll see."

We spent so many hours sitting in coffee shops or taking strolls on a university campus, discussing the woes and rewards of teaching, spirituality, philosophy, and the prodigious ideas of Aristotle, Thomas Aquinas, Mortimer Adler, and many others.

Your example of love and devotion to your wife and two sons remains unparalleled in my experience.

Thank you for being so much more than a friend, colleague, and mentor. All labels fall short of giving you your due. You retired and passed on before I could repay what you gave me, not that I ever really could. I would like you to know that in my thirty-three years of teaching at our school, I tried to live up to your standards of intellect, scholarship, grace, humility, labor, and unfailing compassion and advocacy for students. I tried my best to honor your stout legacy by "paying it forward."

Godspeed in whatever realm you inhabit now. I envision a day when I can shake your hand again, give you a hug, and sit down to resume our conversation about all the things you loved so dearly and were so knowledgeable about: history, art, literature, film, musical theater, religion, philosophy, and pedagogy. You were a true Renaissance man, earning a degree in engineering, deeply knowledgeable about math and science, equally wise about the arts and, most of all, an expert in human kindness. I still stand in the light of your enlightenment.

CHAPTER 30:
The Making of a Writing Teacher

DEAR BEV BANKS,

Thank you for welcoming me into a community of educators who convened several times each school year to evaluate student writing.

I first met you when I was an inexperienced English teacher trying to find his way in a public high school setting. I had the benefit of a strong theoretical foundation in the importance of writing in students' academic growth. However, the reality of working daily with 175 students and getting them to write something of value and then providing them with timely feedback to enable them to increase the value of their writing is an overwhelmingly daunting task. Where does one begin and how does one find the time to read so many ungrammatical sentences and incomplete and/or ill-conceived thoughts and do something concrete to make them better?

This challenge is sufficient to drive new teachers from the profession or to cause less conscientious teachers to assign meaningless writing exercises and then provide only cursory feedback: "Great effort; well done; interesting; keep up the good work; you're really improving!"

Worse yet are the teachers who turn away from the effort and time required to teach writing by assigning paragraphs instead of essays and quick writes that are graded on the basis of completion rather than content and without targeted feedback.

Through the first third of my teaching career, you led my school district's efforts to establish writing standards and assessment practices to ensure that students would be able to write competently by the time they graduated from high school. You directly trained hundreds upon hundreds of teachers like me, and thus indirectly trained hundreds more as we returned to our school sites and shared what we had learned from you.

Your approach was simple yet profound. First you had us examine closely a single evaluation tool, called a rubric in education circles, in order to really understand the intricacies of each score on a five-point scale. You had us spend most of our time discussing the difference between a minimally passing score and a failing score, as this dividing line would determine whether a student qualified for high school graduation or not.

Next, you had us read and score student essays from past years and compare our scores with the other twenty or so teachers sitting at the table and to scores given by previous teachers. This process, called norming, serves as an excellent way to ensure that teachers are grading in a consistent, fair, and uniform manner. As students, we all know how difficult it is to hit a moving target and to adapt to different standards from one teacher to the next.

Once our community of teachers reached agreement on appropriate scores, you then insisted that we write the essay that we were going to assign to our students. What a powerful way to make sure teachers know the difficulties students face, and what an effective way to make sure our evaluations are unbiased and realistic.

Only after all of that did you allow us to read and score current student essays.

As a new teacher, the process you established and the discussions that ensued constituted one of the most influential and valuable training experiences of my entire career. Your work served as a guard against incompetence, uncertainty, and arbitrariness.

As a result of your expertise, I became a much better teacher. I was personally and professionally enriched by the efforts you facilitated to create a truly collaborative community of educators. Learning from one's peers is invaluable. You also made the task of teaching students to write much more manageable and effective. I cannot overstate the debt of gratitude I owe you. If my students knew the positive impact you had on me as an educator, I have every confidence that they would thank you as well.

You are personally responsible for thousands upon thousands of students entering adult life with all the discreet and measurable skills necessary for writing to be deemed competent: critical thinking; clear and cohesive expression; logical organization; development of ideas; support of ideas with reasoning and evidence; correct grammatical structure. You also deserve credit for improving the teaching ability of countless teachers.

What a profound and indispensable contribution you have made to the perpetuation of a literate citizenry.

DEAR SUPPORTERS OF TEACHERS EVERYWHERE,

Teaching is not a part-time or fallback vocation, as some people characterize it with condescension and derision dripping from their words. It is not a vocation at all. Rather, it is a calling, a secular ministry, a devotion to humanity and civilization that is at once debilitating and invigorating in its intricacies and mysteries.

Good teaching is equal parts art, science, empathy, compassion, optimism, nurturing, equanimity, and unyielding, undying belief.

It is an endeavor that depends in large measure on an individual's conscientiousness and innate desire to transform ignorance into knowledge, laziness into arduous effort, pensiveness into confidence, doubt into faith, pessimism into optimism, finite valleys into limitless horizons. It is an endeavor that links past, present, and future and affirms great, timeless human achievement with the possibility of even greater achievement.

Despite all attempts to make teaching a collaborative act, the reality is that when a classroom door closes and a bell signals the start of class, a teacher is alone with students and conscience becomes the ultimate determiner of effort, approach, and efficacy.

Teachers operate most of the time without accurate feedback on their efficacy. Test scores do not tell the full story of how well a teacher is performing or how profoundly a teacher is positively influencing and awakening students.

Assessing whether students are actually learning is endlessly enigmatic and mystifying. Students who appear to be paying attention and processing lessons may in fact only be playing the game and relying on prior knowledge. Conversely, students who appear not to be listening or complying or processing lessons may in fact be internally making great intellectual progress; they just don't display their learning in teacher-created and institutionally sanctioned assessments. There is also the question of when learning actually takes place. It may occur after an assessment is given. One also needs to consider that student performance may only reflect shallow, short-term understanding that will dissipate within days or weeks. None of this is an excuse for poor teaching. It is simply recognition of the intangibles involved in learning.

People who trust and support teachers understand this. They know as parents that children learn and evolve in their own time frame. The effects of lessons taught are frequently delayed, or triggered by additional future learning. Teachers are cogs in an ever-expanding wheel. Teachers are catalysts whose influence and effect cannot accurately and fully be measured. The act of teaching is an act of faith.

Supporters of teachers understand that teachers are motivated by their love for students, by their willingness to suffer through the failure that is an inevitable part of the process of teaching and learning, by an obsessive desire to facilitate students' personal and academic growth, by a willingness to react with compassion to students' immaturity, and ultimately by an aspiration to enhance and accelerate the quality of students' lives and the humanity of their natures.

To all of the parents and community members that have supported me throughout my teaching career, thank you. Your support has meant so much and has made an immeasurably positive difference.

CHAPTER 32:
Essential Colleagues

DEAR FELLOW TEACHERS,

You know that the world is improved incrementally; you know that civilizations are built one child at a time. You respect parents as the first essential builders, and as teachers, you take up the work to ensure that each child is well prepared to inherit the responsibilities necessary to perpetuate the building. You know that embedded in your title as fifth-grade teacher or science teacher, you are fundamentally a construction worker. Your jobsite is a civilized world.

As teachers, your efforts are motivated and guided by a recognition that each student constitutes his or her own microcosm of civilization, to a greater or lesser degree, and either progresses or regresses, evolves or devolves. You willfully bear the boundless burden and challenge to discover, inspire, embellish, enflame, extend, and maximize each person's capacity for progress and evolution. Without your contributions as teachers, the formation and continuation of a civilized macrocosm, whether we define it as a neighborhood, community, society, nation, or world, is immeasurably imperiled.

I want to thank all of my fellow teachers whom I had the honor and privilege of working with over the course of a thirty-three-year career in a public high school. I miss being a part of that collective conscience that is driven to maximize the potential of every precious minute of instructional time by engaging all students in richly valuable learning experiences, despite the fact that the job is confounding, exhaustive, and sometimes impossible.

Whatever success I experienced as a teacher resulted largely from being helped by my fellow teachers. Teaching can be an extraordinarily lonely exercise unless one invites and incorporates input from other teachers. The best schools facilitate teacher-to-teacher teamwork. The best teachers seek it out instinctively and without the urgings of administrators and institutional directives. I'm grateful for all the help I was given by dedicated teachers who were so generous with their time, patience, knowledge, experience, and suggestions.

Teaching involves trial and error, experimentation, and failure. The odds of a new teacher developing into a master teacher are enormously improved through partnerships with other teachers. Throughout my career, I was the beneficiary of such partnerships. I became a better teacher by talking to my peers, asking them how they did things, watching them teach, and getting constructive criticism from teachers who watched me.

I offer my heartfelt thanks to all of my colleagues who vastly enriched my teaching efficacy, and who made me a better human being as well.

DEAR JACK SCHULZE,

You did not impress me when I was introduced to you as the principal of the high school where I had been hired. You struck me as strangely diffident, detached, and unmoved. Your handshake was partial and limp; I got my hand back without any sensation of having been touched. Your eye contact was glancing. Our first conversation was brief, superficial, and impersonal. I left the campus thinking I had made a mistake in accepting the teaching job that had been offered to me, first by a recruiter who was the principal of another school in the district, and then by a district personnel director. I thought because you had not been the one to hire me, perhaps you were divested of my presence or success in your school.

I learned much later that you implicitly trusted the two people who recommended my hire and you felt it unnecessary during our first meeting to conduct a third interview or evaluation of me.

First impressions can be notoriously misleading, and mine of you certainly proved that adage. I want to thank you for the decade-long second impression you made on me.

You turned out to be the most personal leader imaginable.

As a new teacher, I spent quite a few weekends on campus decorating my classroom, writing lesson plans, figuring out grading systems, reading student essays, and generally trying to gain my footing as a symbol of structure, standards, knowledge, and wisdom for a wildly diverse collection of 200 energetic and attention-seeking teenagers.

You lived two golf shots from our school and it's not an exaggeration to say that you spent more time on campus than you did at home. You typically spent Saturdays at our school, tending to your beloved rose bushes, gathering tumbleweeds, picking up trash, and clearing paperwork from your enormous desk.

As I would arrive for my personally imposed Saturday shift, I could count on seeing your beat-up Dodge Ram work truck in the parking lot. The floorboards were covered with all manner of construction tools; the truck's bed was filled with shovels, pruning shears, pick-axes, and other assorted gardening tools.

With your clothes stained with sweat and your face ruddy from exertion, you engaged me in personal, meaningful conversations about myself, how my teaching was progressing, experiences with students, and concerns about our school that I would like to see addressed.

I quickly learned that you were at your best in these informal settings. You were always unassuming, soft spoken, and kind, empathetic when I voiced frustrations, and joyful when I reported good things, especially regarding students. You could not have been prouder of the institution you led as principal for over a quarter-century. You could not have been a more ardent defender of your beloved school. It was your vocation, your avocation, your church, and your home.

Late at night and on Sunday afternoons, you frequently cruised through the campus hallways in your chocolate brown Mercedes 450SL making sure all windows and doors were battened down tight and no intruders were lurking to cause mischief. Under your watch, not a single trashcan was out of place. Not a single item of sports equipment was left forgotten on a field.

You had a hard-working, reliable, competent maintenance crew, but your conscience commanded you to personally oversee every inch of the campus with your own eyes.

You were our school's most enthusiastic champion and quite assertive in rebutting and addressing criticisms.

Your philosophy as a school principal was to hire the best people possible, give them the tools and support they needed to be successful, and then get out of their way.

Thank you for the trust and faith you placed in me as an educator. You provided me with space, time, and autonomy to grow as an educator and I'm deeply grateful.

You treated me like a son, and your fatherly instincts were exceptionally good. You put your arm around my shoulder literally and figuratively on many occasions, lifting up my sagging spirits and tickling my funny bone with silly jokes. You loved to share puns, and no matter how woeful mine were, you never failed to smile and laugh.

You are a preeminent example of one who gave his life to the people and work that mattered to him the most. For being that exemplar for me and countless others, thank you.

CHAPTER 34:
Heroic Leadership

DEAR BLANCA CAVAZOS,

You were appointed principal of my school upon the death of the man who had been principal for nearly three decades. That fact alone represents a monumental challenge. Change is usually hard, but change so long delayed is excruciatingly difficult.

You were fully aware of the daunting task you faced, and you were more than equal to the challenge. But there would be other challenges that you could not foresee. You would prove ready to meet those as well.

As a teacher who worked for you and with you during your tenure as principal, I thank you for your unwavering friendship, support, courage, moral defiance, leadership, integrity, and your willingness to be the hardest working person on campus, which is what a principal must be in order to set the right example, overcome the unrelenting stream of high-pressured challenges, and ultimately be successful.

Perhaps the most important and revealing statement I can make about you is that you enrolled your three sons in the school you were principal of. Based on geography, your sons were scheduled to attend a different high school, in close proximity to your home. But you enrolled your sons in your school, not primarily because you wanted to keep a close watch on them but because you believed that your school would provide them with the most effective and enriching education possible. Not a perfect education, but a deeply meaningful one that would prepare them for adulthood. You entrusted the school that you were leading with your own children, the three most important people in your life. I can think of no better symbol of your deep faith in our school than believing in its capacity to provide your own flesh and blood with everything that a school should provide all students: nurturing, safety, academic rigor, personal enrichment, and a gateway to a meaningful, worthwhile, consequential, and rewarding life. I heard you say on many occasions to other students, parents, and community members that you believed in our school so much that you specifically chose to send your own children to it. There can be no better validation of a school's value. A teacher can ask of a principal no greater commitment to a school's integrity and efficacy than that.

In the earliest days of your tenure as principal, one of our students was killed in an off-campus shooting, presenting you with a far greater challenge than merely taking over for a beloved predecessor who had a core of staff members reluctant to transfer their allegiance to a new leader. The circumstances of the shooting were shocking and heart wrenching. The murder was a premeditated act involving kidnapping and an execution-style shooting in a nearby agricultural field. Needless to say, our community of students, parents, staff members, and stakeholders was devastated, and you were the point person to lead us all through an extended period of mourning, the slow unfolding of the gruesome details of the murder, the agonizing period of waiting for justice to be rendered, and the impossible task of consoling the inconsolable. You proved to be exactly the right person at exactly the right time. Through your tireless work ethic, your abiding sense of love for and loyalty to our school and community, and your decency and humanity, you compassionately and competently guided our school through this nightmarish experience. When we were all at our limit of tending to wounded souls, you were still sitting with students and parents in your office or on a school bench, offering wise counsel and a tender heart, answering the most delicate and difficult telephone calls, dealing with the media, and maintaining our school's integrity as a place of learning. You reminded everyone that schools have an obligation not only to educate minds but also to protect and nurture vulnerable hearts, especially in the midst of searing pain.

Some principals are managers; some are instructional leaders. You were both at a time when our school needed both. You became our principal when California, as well as many other states, was going through yet another period of education reform, transitioning from accounting for seat time to reestablishing discreet learning standards at each grade level and developing ways to measure whether those standards were being met by individual students and schools as a whole. It fell to you to guide us through this new phase of standardized testing and school accountability measures. Once again, your steady leadership and profound knowledge of instructional practices made you exactly the right person at exactly the right time.

Schools are strange and unique structures, weighed down mightily by bureaucracy, political ideology, personal whims, wrongheaded perceptions, teacher tenure, and a reward system based too often on seniority and subservience rather than merit and creativity. Sadly, there sometimes exists a "go along to get along" mentality in schools that can demoralize the most conscientious teachers and strangle the institution's capacity to provide students with the best education possible. You challenged all of those negative elements and "rattled the cages" of the entrenched power structures, all for the betterment of students. You created a vision for our school, challenged staff to buy in or get out, fought tirelessly to create optimum learning conditions for students, and always held the best interests of our students, parents, and staff members close to your heart.

You consistently demonstrated the courage to look people in the eye and implore them to "step up their game" for those who matter the most in schools: the students. You aggressively rejected the notion that schools were chiefly lifetime employment vehicles for people who were content to go through the motions, put on a good show, collect a paycheck, and cynically initiate a countdown to summer vacation on the first day of school. You demanded results—namely evidence of significant student learning.

Thank you for your principled leadership, your earnest desire to meet the most formidable challenges head on with every ounce of your energy, strength, talent, intelligence, and humanity, your steadfast commitment to improving the lives of all students, and your unwavering commitment to increasing the effectiveness of the entire educational community.

DEAR CYNTHIA BRAKEMAN,

You were my sister-in-arms.

Our battlefield was the American landscape of institutional education called high school.

We worked together for twenty years as English teacher colleagues at Arvin High School in California's Kern High School District. For much of that time, our careers intertwined as English Department co-chairs.

I want to thank you for your friendship, for your collegiality, but most of all, for your stout, unwavering example of what a teacher should be: empowering, empathetic, and driven beyond the limits of time and energy to help every student—regardless of attitude, ability, motivation, or behavior—develop to the fullest extent possible as people and life-long learners.

You empowered every student who entered your sphere of influence. You awakened those who were intellectually asleep. You instilled direction and purpose in those who were stalled or coasting, numb to passing time and life's challenges. You inculcated self-confidence in those who had given up on themselves. You enabled students to grow as readers and writers. You prepared students for higher goals and achievement. You held students to the ideals of honor, civility, morality, and authentic effort.

I know from sharing a classroom with you that you scoured every syllable your students wrote in essays and research papers, providing invaluable feedback necessary to engender writing improvement. You understood that practice without precise, detailed feedback was worthless.

From the outset of your teaching career, you challenged students to read books—not trendy young adult titles with fleeting themes and impact, but high quality literature written by masters such as V. S. Naipaul, Joseph Conrad, and Chinua Achebe. You created a reading list that had the potential to widen students' narrow perspectives, expand their cultural literacy, and open their minds to ideas that otherwise would elude them. You desperately wanted students who matriculated at four-year universities to be able to converse and compete with their well-read peers.

You ardently fought against the recent movement in high schools away from requiring students to read full-length books and toward nonfiction articles, as if literature had lost its value.

You religiously taught students how to write research papers, knowing that college professors would expect students had learned all the discrete skills the process entailed.

Countless students returned while in college or after earning their degrees to let you know that their success was due in large measure to your teaching—a testament to the enduring impact you had on students.

You enthusiastically embraced the challenge of becoming an instructional leader, knowing that such a position brings extra responsibility without actual power (knowing also that a department chair is a glorified cat-herder). Teachers, especially English teachers, can be an obstinate, egotistical bunch, often unwilling to bend to group norms and goals. And even when English teachers do agree to comply with overall plans and objections, they do so with resistance, objections, and caveats. You also understood that a department chair is frequently a human shield, standing between teachers and administrators, between teachers and counselors, caught in the crossfire of competing needs and objectives. You were a formidable shield, willing to absorb attacks from all sides.

As a department chair, you increased the potency and efficacy of every colleague you worked with. To those who were content with mediocrity, you awakened a conscience. To those who selfishly pursued personal aims and peeves, you planted and nurtured seeds of loyalty to communal goals. To those who resisted good teaching practices, you argued, pleaded, cajoled, demonstrated, modeled, insisted, and sometimes badgered.

You never once shied away from directly confronting enemies in school such as: individual and institutional resistance to learning; restrictive bell schedules and calendars based on tradition and convenience rather than students' needs; the misuse and manipulation of data to maintain the pretense of academic progress and hide failure; the oppression of politically driven testing practices disconnected from true academic achievement; the inhumanity of overcrowded classrooms obliterating the individual attention desperately needed by so many students; the sacrifice of scared instructional time to feed the bureaucratic beast.

In the midst of the academic content standards movement during the 1990s, through endless discussions with politicians and administrators and colleagues about what we, as English teachers, should be teaching, you simplified the answer to an irrefutable essence: our efforts should be laser-focused on helping students become better thinkers, readers, and writers. Every other discussion was about *how*, not *what*.

In your twenty years of teaching, you were so much more than a master teacher, although that would have been enough. You were the conscience of the school. You were the "go-to" person when tensions were running high, advice was needed, and tough decisions had to be made. You were soldierly in your willingness to put it all on the line, regardless of the personal cost. You were stalwart in your devotion to educational ideals—ever ready to roll your sleeves up and work tirelessly until the job was done.

Upon your retirement after two decades in finance and two decades in education, you opted to leave your well-earned easy chair unoccupied and to run for our high school district's board of trustees. You wanted to bring to the school board a teacher's perspective, which was sorely lacking at the time. You thankfully won a seat on the board and are now preparing for another election.

Having you as a colleague was a profound blessing. You helped me become a better person and better teacher. Having you serve our community as a school board member gives me hope that the current generation of students moving through our schools will be well prepared to navigate the stormy waters of the twenty-first century.

PART EIGHT: PARENTS

DEAR MOTHER,

Please forgive me for my selfish transgressions. When I consider some of the things I've done, causing you interminable consternation that you absolutely didn't deserve, I long for the cleansing of a formal Catholic confession.

I think I was in first grade when I displayed unreasonable spite—both of myself and of you—which, some sixty years later, still causes me mortifying embarrassment. I was getting ready to walk to my school bus stop, and for some inexplicable reason, I decided to leave my hair in a state of unholy mess. You instructed me to return to the bathroom and apply a sticky, wax-like substance that pushed up in a hard plastic tube like a deodorant stick. A little of the substance went a long way. In a fit of anger, I decided to smear the waxy material over my head in a paroxysm of exaggeration. I have no reason why. Popular at the time, I had been using the substance on a regular basis for weeks. It gave my curly hair a bit of much needed shape and firmness. I walked out of the bathroom as if nothing out of the ordinary had occurred, when in fact my head was covered with deep layers of wax, to the point of ridiculousness. I was almost out the door when you noticed my handiwork. I can't imagine what went through your mind. I don't have to imagine how you reacted. You pulled me back into the house, stripped me of my lunch, book-bag, and clothing, and gave me what would now be called an old-fashioned whippin'. Then you threw me into bed, with a non-negotiable warning to remain there for the day.

What causes me such regret and shame all these years later is how you felt guilty for such a long time afterwards for the punishment you enacted. Trying to balance your guilt with your outrage at my inexplicable behavior made you cry as you walloped me.

Many years later, I ask you if you remember the incident and you say, "Of course. I can still see the layers of wax sitting on your head like cement." You apologize for your self-described "overreaction." I apologize again for my immaturity. You explain that what irritated you the most was my expectation that the nuns and students at school would have been subjected to looking at my absurd appearance throughout the day. You were also incensed that I was willing to reflect so poorly on my family; you legitimately felt that your reputation as a parent, as well as my father's, was at stake.

How I wish I could go back in time and make a different choice in that bathroom with that silly hair product. My behavior was small and petty. Your guilt was large and debilitating.

As Mark Twain pointed out, the past really does humiliate. Thank you for giving me the punishment I truly deserved.

DEAR FATHER,

Thank you for tolerating my childhood impetuosity and my need to distance myself from you through far too much of my life. I suppose the immaturity I displayed in my youth was nothing out of the ordinary, but I'm grateful that you bore it with undying love, especially when it challenged your deeply held sense of decorum and close-to-the-heart principles.

Growing up as you did with depression-era hardship, and sacrifice a staple of daily life, I know you were baffled that I was so slow to appreciate your determination to provide your family with as much ease and opportunity as possible. I was too busy trying to carve out my own identity to notice, and for too long, I lacked the graciousness to be more overtly thankful for the way you tried to shield me from harm, lack of opportunity, and errors of judgment.

Perhaps what I'm feeling is nothing more than every son's and daughter's regrets about childhood indiscretions, but I long to share my feelings with you now to assure you that when I was growing up, despite my outward signs of displeasure and disappointment, you did all the big things right. As an adult, I tried to convey my appreciation of you, but I'm sometimes wracked with doubt that I was convincing enough. I would like to have another opportunity to thank you, to tell you that I finally understand that who you were was lovingly and inordinately about who I would become, and I'm eternally grateful for that.

I seek comfort by telling myself that I was able to close our sometimes broken circle by becoming the person that you wanted me to become, which turned out to be the person that I ultimately wanted to become. All the distance I put between us as my unalienable right was so unnecessary. You were accommodating and understanding in the end; I just didn't know how to ask you for what I needed.

I would like to share a home with you again and coexist like men on a mutually agreed upon and satisfying mission, determined to delight in the simple things and face the big things side by side, arm in arm, values and principles intertwined and ready for peace or storm.

In my mind, I return again and again to my decision to accept a teaching job in Japan. My desire to live and work in another country was something that perplexed you and caused you great worry. But you supported my decision and insisted on driving me to LAX for my early-morning flight. We rose at 2 AM and were on the freeway by 3.

You drove with such purpose, facilitating my need to separate myself from you, to find my own path, to construct my own identity. You stood at the boarding gate, keeping watch, extending your arm in a goodbye salute, and letting me know that you would be there for me upon my return.

Through all the intervening years, you wrote letters expressing your love by talking about US politics and baseball, longing for my well-being, and assuring me that I would find what I was looking for. A son could not have asked for anything more.

I hope this attempt to say thank you is an echo of what I was able to convey while you were still here saluting me, keeping watch, and awaiting my return.

DEAR MOTHER,

Thank you for acting as a buffer between my father and me whenever we butted heads, which regrettably was often throughout my teenage years. You defended me in our disagreements and arguments and shielded me from his disappointment and anger, all at great personal cost to yourself. It took me far too long to realize that you paid a heavy price for sticking up for me. Long after he and I had reconciled, my father would hold on to his disappointment in you and direct his lingering wrath toward you. His weapons were silence and temper tantrums. Unfortunately, you endured countless days of silence and bore the worst of my father's outbursts, which in many instances were about me, not you.

Your nature was always to be nonconfrontational, but there were times when you could not hold your opinion and maintain your internal peace.

I deeply regret that I was slow to figure out how to keep you out of dust-ups with my father, especially since they were typically about unimportant matters, such as my hair length and style of dress. My insistence on letting my hair grow well below my collar and wearing ragged jeans and tennis shoes cost you dearly. If only I could go back in time and conform to my father's reasonable standards, and thereby save you from much anguish and grief.

It seems irrational to wish that the conflicts between my father and me had been more substantial and thereby commensurate with the suffering you endured. But I confess that I sometimes thought that way, and still do, irrationally wishing for more severe conflict, especially when I'm feeling guilty about the way you were drawn into our battles.

On occasions when you defended me, or simply tried to reframe my grievances as only a mother could, you paid a stiff price. If you remained silent, he assumed you were taking my side, and the price for you was equally stiff. My father was quick to forgive me, but forgiveness for you was excruciatingly slow.

If only I had wised up sooner, acted in a less selfish manner, and thought of your mental and emotional health more than my own petty preferences.

I'm not naïve to think that I was responsible for all the issues and grievances that you and my father dealt with as a married couple. But I know that I sometimes served as extra wood on fires that were already smoldering. I'm profoundly sorry and forever grateful for your love and sacrifice. I hope that I was able to earn the forgiveness that you gave me before I deserved it.

DEAR FATHER,

You were my first and most important teacher throughout my life, and since your death, your lessons have only grown in importance and influence.

When I was old enough to analyze your presence, you were a force of nature. Your body was expansive, imposing, and undeniable, like a redwood tree. You were stout and solid in the way you occupied space and held your ground.

I could not imagine a way around you—much less through or over you. Your voice commanded me like a drill sergeant's, impossible to ignore or defy. At the same time, it reassured me that you were in control, and I would learn how to acquire control and power for myself by following your directions.

When I was three or four years old, you would wrestle with me in your bed. At some point, you would raise one arm straight up and tempt me to pull it down or knock it over. Your arm proved immovable and later symbolized for me your physicality and resiliency. Although you were short in stature, five feet and seven inches, your body was thick with wiry muscles, shaped by the five years you spent toiling in a steel mill, much of the time pushing a wheelbarrow loaded down with scraps of iron. Those years honed your body into iron flesh.

Your body mirrored your intellect, which was fortified with iron-hard principles that you used as guideposts for your life journey and imposed upon me.

You taught me to read, using the *Pittsburgh-Post Gazette* and our local newspaper, *The Mon-Valley Independent,* as texts. You had no time or tolerance for children's books. You wanted me to read about the news of the day, politics, the arts, and sports.

As I matured, your lessons in reading comprehension, main ideas, supporting details, argumentation, persuasion, and vocabulary evolved into long discussions while we were seated side by side on the couch, in the car, at the dinner table, or in a coffee shop. We became allies in the effort to make sense of the world through a rigorous examination of history, government figures, policies, social trends, and political philosophies.

You provided me with a subscription to the *Saturday Review* magazine, which was dense with articles about society, politics, literature, and film written by serious journalists and scholars representing all fields of human knowledge. You wanted me to conduct my own independent research so I would bring discussion topics to you that you hadn't initiated. You delighted in me finding articles and bringing them to you and then sharing our reactions and opinions.

We watched movies and engaged in our own version of Siskel and Ebert, two preeminent film critics in the eighties, nineties, and two thousands. You introduced me to film's Golden Age of actors: Clark Gable, Bette Davis, Gary Cooper, James Stewart, Jean Harlow, Claudette Colbert, Jane Russell, Humphrey Bogart, and so on. You also immersed me in your beloved "B" western stars: Gene Autry,

Ken Maynard, Tom Mix, Bob Steele, and Roy Rogers, among many others.

You took me to see John F. Kennedy speak at a campaign stop in our hometown when I was young enough to sit on your shoulders. We spent hours in the Nixon Library reliving political campaigns and conventions, the Vietnam War (you served two tours of duty in that conflict), the president's détente with Russia and China, the Kent State shootings, and of course Watergate.

When I was growing up, you became a symbol of hard work, honesty, and integrity, and these words represented you all your life, without fail. When something needed to be accomplished, you showed up early and were always the last one to leave. You were the ironman rowing the boat and shielding everyone from the crashing waves. In the face of long odds and doubtful victory, you were eager to take on the task, come what may. Setbacks only made you more determined.

When I was going through my years of rebellion, you were initially an intractable force who, after a few years of grinding struggle and conflict that consumed us both, gradually relented and allowed me to experiment, to fail, to make some bad choices. You loved me through all of that and welcomed reconciliation without animosity or grudges.

You supported me through everything I ever tried and accepted the choices I made, even when you would have chosen differently. I know that some of my entanglements were especially hard for you to fathom or endure, such as my stints as a janitor, a golf course maintenance crew member, and a college-educated handyman for the local Boys and Girls Club.

But you always helped me get up when life landed a square one on my jaw and put me on my backside.

As I twisted and turned my tortuous way into adulthood, you gave me all the respect one could ever ask for, more respect than I deserved.

Growing up, you never let me leave the house without a few twenty-dollar bills in my pocket. You wanted me to be prepared for emergencies and contingency plans. Even as an adult, the first thing you did when I visited was go with me to a gas station to fill up my tank. Later, in the garage, we would check the oil, other fluid levels, and tire pressure. My age didn't matter to you. You were making sure your son was driving a well-equipped, safe vehicle. These gestures were your way of saying, without words, "I love you."

As I reflect on all our shared history, I realize with profound appreciation how most of your life was spent preparing others for whatever tomorrow would deliver—good, bad, or indifferent. You were constantly asking me what I was doing today to be ready for tomorrow.

I used to tease you when I was older about your fixation with your file cabinet that contained all your documents describing in precise details how you wanted us to handle your passing and what steps we needed to take to process insurance, social security, and pension benefits. You had the phone numbers listed and all contact information clearly displayed. The steps we would need to take were meticulously outlined in sequential order. You always insisted that I review everything with you on each and every visit.

You made decisions about your funeral and burial years in advance so others wouldn't have to experience such trauma. You had decided on cremation and interment at Riverside National Cemetery. You saved your family from having to make all the difficult decisions upon your passing, including the urn that you wanted your ashes placed in. You wrote out in explicit detail what you wanted on your stone marker. You wanted to save your family from having to mourn and make tough decisions at the same time. This was the penultimate example of you making sure that you were ready for the penultimate tomorrow that we all must face.

A few weeks before you died, you called me into your den and sat me down for one final lesson. You said matter-of-factly, "I'm done."

You would not be making any more trips out of the house, you would not be running any more errands, you would not be making any more visits to family or friends, and you would have no further need for your vehicle.

You put to rest any lingering disagreements or conflicts between us, though there were none. We had done that work many years before. But you made it clear that none of that mattered, then or now. You told me that I was the son you had always wanted. You trusted me that I had learned all the lessons that you had tried to teach me. You told me that I would know what to do. Then you asked me to help you put on your socks and slippers so you would be ready for your tomorrow.

In hospice, when you were very near the end, you sat looking at the grain of a wooden door. You saw images of yourself and my mother in the grain, side by side, intertwined. It was the image that you held onto until you could hold it no more.

To say that I am thankful and grateful for everything you taught me is much too much of an understatement. To say that I love you more now than ever before is also a woefully inadequate declaration. I am still learning your lessons, working hard to help others and myself be prepared for what tomorrow may bring, and making sure I am ready for my penultimate tomorrow.

CHAPTER 40:
Selfless

DEAR MOTHER,

You lived for your children. Our world was your world. The home you created was first and foremost a setting to make us comfortable, keep us safe, and meet our needs. Yes, you decorated it to your liking, but everything was arranged and maintained to support us. You provided us with a secure, stable space in which to grow, throw fits, hide out, dream, worry, panic, plan, and ultimately to use as a model and springboard to create our own nurturing spaces.

When your daughter grew into adulthood, you were content to let her relationship with you evolve more into a sisterhood, though of course you never stopped being her mother. But you let her take the lead in so many ways. You let her become your teacher, your conduit through which you could experience things that otherwise you would have missed, occupied as you were with caring for and supporting your husband. You two shopped together, cooked together, entertained together, vacationed together, lamented husbands' shortcomings together, helped rear grandchildren and great-grandchildren together, laughed together, grieved together, and philosophized together.

With brief exceptions, you lived close together and saw each other or talked virtually every day of your lives. You enjoyed a sacred, unbreakable unity with your daughter that seems to be more typical of a much earlier century.

For me, you were a much-needed shield against my father's occasional fits of anger and harsh judgment. You were my refuge in times of distress and hopelessness as I tried to navigate the deep waters of my father's expectations. Without your buffer, I'm not sure how I would have survived. You didn't always have answers, but you always listened and empathized. You always gave me a feeling that we would endure together in times of crises.

Thank you for your marvelous example of how a parent can evolve to accommodate and support their children's evolution, and for your unwavering, undying love.

DEAR FATHER,

Embarking on a road trip with you led to so many eye-opening and life-altering discoveries and realizations that I never could have predicted and that I am forever thankful for. The ten-day experience is something that I'll never be able to relive often enough.

It started out casually and evolved into something poignant and indelible. While on a weekend visit with you and mom, you expressed an interest in making "one last trip" to our hometown of Monessen, Pennsylvania. You were in your early eighties, in relatively good health despite two hip replacement operations, and thought the time was ripe for such an excursion. You had one remaining brother, a sister, two brothers-in-law, and several nieces and nephews that you wanted to see. You also wanted to see what had become of Monessen, a once charming town twenty miles outside of Pittsburgh and now denigrated by a collapsed steel industry.

Mom stated defiantly that she had no interest in returning home.

You could not understand her disinterest in seeing "for the last time" her two brothers and her own neighboring hometown of Charleroi. You viewed connecting with your brother as a moral necessity and your wife's lack of a complementary need dumbfounded and disappointed you profoundly. Her resistance continued, despite your determination to make the journey, causing you great disappointment.

I sat with you both as the discussion ensued and tried to play the role of arbiter, exploring the dangers of one making the trip without the other and the benefits of you traveling together. In retrospect, my arguments to change my mother's perspective seem clichéd and naïve. "This may be your last opportunity to see your two brothers [a third was deceased], the house you grew up in, the town of your origin, your surviving relatives through marriage." To no avail, I further argued, "After spending a few days with family, you and dad can take a few side trips to New York, Philadelphia, Washington, DC, wherever you'd like. You are both in good health, but you don't know how long that will be the case; take advantage of that before it's too late."

My mother remained wholly un-persuaded. My talking only hardened her resistance and deepened your dejection at being rebuffed.

Deterred but not defeated, I tried a different tack. I said that I would accompany you in my mother's absence. I couched it in terms of a "father-and-son road trip." I think you and my mother were caught off guard. I was sincere in my offer to go, but I was also hoping that Mom would feel left out and change her mind. She did not, much to your dismay.

In my mind, I quickly began citing the reasons why my idea had merit. I would be able to insulate you from all the annoyances of planning and executing the trip: airline, rental car, and hotel reservations; working out an itinerary to satisfy your objectives (you also wanted to visit a life-long friend who was living in Philadelphia);

handling currency (this was the era of cashier's checks); hauling luggage; doing the driving.

Once you realized that mom was not going to change her mind, you accepted my offer to accompany you. As you were never one to easily relinquish control under any circumstances, you surprised me by letting me make all the necessary arrangements.

We planned to make the trip in late June, so we had about six weeks to prepare. You asked me to keep you apprised of the progress I was making in taking care of all the details. While I felt honored that you were granting me this responsibility, I knew it came with a price—namely that you would insist on knowing each arrangement I made in a timely manner. You would have numerous questions and you would need proof and assurances that I had done what I reported to have done, in the form of hard evidence—confirmation numbers, tickets, and so on. This became a source of frustration for you and humor for me.

We made this trip just as the twenty-first century had dawned. Technology was changing how transactions were made, less so for one of your generation who was having trouble adapting to our *Brave New World*. As an example, I purchased our direct flight airline tickets online, acquired specific seat assignments, and printed out our boarding passes. When I conveyed this to you, filled with self-satisfaction that all our flight data was settled and locked in, you were confused by these new procedures and frustrated that I could not produce actual tickets in the form you were accustomed to. You quickly adopted a mantra of "Show me the tickets." I understood your discomfort and doubt and did my best to assure you that everything was fine. But absent physical tickets, you were hopelessly frustrated and panicked. Showing you confirmation emails, electronic banking charges, and boarding passes printed on my home computer did nothing to assuage your concerns. You looked at electronic messages as if they were hieroglyphics. You held boarding passes in your hands as if they were counterfeit. You actually thought I had been swindled.

Even after we had boarded the plane and were sitting in our seats, buckled in for takeoff, you expected a flight attendant to tap us on the shoulder and instruct us to deplane since we didn't have authentic tickets to prove our right to our seats. Even in the air, you were asking, "What happens if we are asked to show our tickets?"

A second source of frustration and humor was money. You asked me how much money I was planning to take. I explained that I saw no need to carry a large stash of cash or to secure travelers checks, since an ATM card meant I could obtain cash virtually anywhere at any time. I preferred the peace of mind that comes with not having so much cash that one worries about keeping it safe. You did not have an ATM card, didn't see the need for one, and thought the concept behind such a card was unnecessary and foolish. Out of respect for your old school mentality, I secured traveler's checks for you.

On the day of our departure, as we were getting ready to drive to Los Angeles International Airport, you handed me $3,000 in cash and told me to take care of it. All these years later, the irony still causes chuckles, but at the time, I was mortified. You wiped out all the peace of mind traveling with a reasonable amount of money was going to afford me. When I asked you where you thought I should place such a cumbersome stack of bills, you gave me a money belt as an answer. Without the wad of bills stuffed inside, your belt didn't fit me; with money, I looked like an overstuffed diner at an all-you-can-eat buffet. I ended up storing the money in my carry-on backpack and never left it out of my sight.

Once airborne, with my backpack wedged tightly between my feet, I tried to calm your fears that we wouldn't have a rental car waiting for us at Pittsburgh International Airport and that we were without hotel reservations in the cities we would be traveling to— Monessen, Philadelphia, and Washington, DC. I failed to assuage your fears, and my failure hurt my heart. I realized too late that I should have involved you in all the arrangements I had made. Relinquishing control to others, even your own son, was so foreign to you.

I apologize for getting snarky on one occasion and saying, "Dad, you'll just have to wait until we're sitting in our rental car and sleeping in our hotel rooms." Most of the time, I tried softly and patiently to calm your concerns. I did not want to provoke you and ruin our trip with rancor just as it was beginning.

Eventually, you seemed to enjoy the five-hour airplane ride cross-country, appreciating the attention from the flight attendant and consuming your meal with gusto. I arranged for us to each have an aisle seat, and you were surprised that one could arrange that. I resisted a temptation to champion the wonders of technology, feeling such a move would be arrogant and gratuitous. I simply said I was happy you were pleased with your seat.

On the ground in Pittsburgh, you grudgingly used a public restroom, something you hated doing. Countless times, I had been out to lunch or to a movie with you when you insisted on waiting until we got back home before using the restroom. This was a peccadillo that I knew you would have to sacrifice on our trip. I stood at the sink and listened to you cursing from inside the stall. This confirmed to me that the sacrifice would be bloody. I was grateful that we had the facility to ourselves.

Walking through Pittsburgh International Airport brought back a flood of memories for you. I could see in your face that you were becoming contemplative and nostalgic. You had spent so much of your life in western Pennsylvania. You looked like you were home. "Dammit. Your mother should be here." There was nothing I could say.

I tried to hurry us along to the rental car counter. As we approached our vehicle, you looked at me with surprise. "A Lincoln Town Car! You went all out. But I don't think we need it." You were impressed—too impressed. You wanted me to return to the counter and exchange it for a smaller, less expensive vehicle. I argued that I wanted us to be comfortable, considering we would be driving across the width of Pennsylvania and down to Washington, DC. You reluctantly relented.

You were anxious to drive directly to your brother Bob's house. Our hotel could wait. Our trip predated GPS technology, so we relied on physical maps. Your brother had sent you directions, taking into consideration all the street repairs PENNDOT (Pennsylvania Department of Transportation) had scheduled. Your brother had said in a letter, "I know you know the way, but you'll have to avoid all the heavy-duty street maintenance or the hour-long drive will expand to all day and you'll end up in Ohio." Armed with your brother Bob's directions and state and city maps, we rolled out in the luxury of the Town Car. You seemed to enjoy the plush leather seat and generous legroom.

PENNDOT threw us many curves that day. I lost count of all the detours from the detours. But we made it.

Although you were in your eighth decade of life, you had a habit of exiting a vehicle while it was still moving. You had done this a number of times when we were running an errand and I was pulling into a parking space. I had lovingly scolded and teased you for your impatience. "Dad, would you mind waiting until the car is at a full stop before getting out?" You would always laugh and say, "Let me do this while I still can." I could not argue with your logic. On this occasion, I could only enjoy your excitement, which compelled you to predictably jump out of the car as I was still parking. Your younger brother Bob came running out of the house with excitement equal to yours, and the two of you embraced for a long time. I stood by the Town Car and wiped away tears, imagining you as kids playing outside and squeezing all the light out of the day before going inside for dinner and bed.

We went inside now, you and your brother still arm in arm, eager to escape the Pennsylvania humidity. Your brother gave us a tour of his charming home. A septuagenarian widower, he kept a tidy house and was proud of his ability to still cut his own lawn. His sloping backyard served as his playground where he fought to maintain his strength, balance, and agility.

I fell into a nostalgic revelry as we climbed down into his basement. I grew up in a house not far from his that also had a basement. It served as a play area and refuge, affording me privacy as I watched shows like *American Bandstand* and *Where the Action Is!* My basement also scared me at night with its dark corners and ground-level windows. My imagination would sometimes get the best of me. I would convince myself that I could see the legs of killers who were preparing to break in and abduct me. In a state of self-generated fright, I used to walk backwards up the stairs and out of imaginary danger. Here, my uncle Bob's cellar looked cozy and well organized.

After we sat for a few minutes in the living room and my father cooled off with a coke, my father made a request. "I'd like to go to the graveyard to see Mum and Papa." My uncle Bob was quick to comply. "Give me a minute to change and I'll be ready to go."

Soon we were kneeling at the gravesite of my grandparents in Monessen's Grandview Cemetery, which overlooks the Monongahela River. Their headstone was decorated with black and white photos of Dominic and Mary Coccari, immigrants from Italy in the early 1900s.

My uncle Bob confessed that he did not visit the gravesite as often as he should. My father and uncle reminisced about their parents, and I listened intently. After thirty minutes or so, my father reluctantly pulled himself away to look for other gravesites of family, friends, and acquaintances.

My father led us on a mission to locate the gravesites of people he had grown up with, attended school with, worked in the steel mill with, and served in the Army with. My uncle and I were astounded by my father's recollection of details surrounding each person. He recited facts about their lives, incidents involving marriages, divorces, and arrests, fights in the schoolyard, and so on. My uncle and I were saturated with stories to the point of exhaustion.

Next to the street, the cemetery is level, but then it slopes down at a precipitous angle to the river. My father insisted on climbing down deep into the hillside in search of gravesites. The three of us were drenched in sweat and getting a real workout. My father seemed to know the majority of people buried throughout. On his search for specific people, he came across names that were familiar to him or that jogged his memory. He would immediately launch into accounts of their lives, as if he had been living in close proximity to them all along.

My uncle cried for mercy as my father peppered him with questions, taxing his memory and zapping his patience and strength. "Jim, I can't remember as well as you." My uncle did, in fact, remember quite a lot; however, he seemed less interested than my father in mining the past. My uncle and I marveled at my father's memory of half-century-old facts and tried to keep up with his trek among the headstones and through history.

After two hours of walking virtually every inch of the cemetery, we dropped my uncle off at his house to rest. My father and I left to check into our hotel, and we planned to meet my uncle later that evening for dinner.

My father was relieved to find that my assurances of our hotel reservation were justified. I took a swim, and he took a nap. Apparently, his march through the cemetery had fatigued him as well.

The early summer heat swarmed and suffocated, but the pool provided soothing and invigorating alleviation. As I swam and splashed around, I thought of how intent my father behaved in the cemetery. He looked like a man possessed by a need to honor all the departed souls he could locate with his remembrances. He seemed to be trying to make up for his decades-long absence in our hometown in a few hurried, sweaty hours. I was worn out by the intensity of the day. Hours later on a poolside recliner, I fell into a brief but deep sleep. I woke to find my father swimming laps. I joined him, and we swam side by side until our bodies could endure no further exertion.

Back in the room, I asked my father if the trip was meeting his expectations. His reply pleased me to no end. "We should have done this sooner." I felt bad that my mother was not sharing this experience.

Thank you, Father and Uncle Bob, for the exceptional example of brotherly love. When you greeted each other, years seemed to fall away, distance melted, and your eyes were bright with love and history.

Thank you, Father, for giving me the opportunity to help you reunite with your family, your roots, and your allegiance to those who came before and to those who influenced you as you grew into adulthood.

CHAPTER 42:
Playing the Cards Dealt

DEAR MOTHER,

You made the best of so many situations that weren't your own choosing. Perhaps that is what we are all faced with doing in this life. We get to make choices some of the time, but most of the time, we must react to the choices others make and find a way to live with them.

Through your humility, grace, capacity to endure oppression, and indefatigable will to find joy in the everyday small things, I would say that you definitely found a way to live a worthy life inside the confines of circumstances beyond your control and within the parameters of other people's choices.

As a young girl, you grew up in poverty, without toys, without a family car, without eyeglasses that you desperately needed. Your father lived most of his life as an undocumented, illegal Russian immigrant in constant fear of deportation. You, your sister, and three rambunctious brothers somehow shared two tiny upstairs bedrooms and a single bathroom with a claw foot tub and no shower. The coal furnace in the cellar three floors below you wasn't strong enough to send heat up to the bedrooms and so you and your siblings had to bury yourselves in a mountain of blankets during the frosty winter months to stay warm. Your house had no air-conditioning, and the only escape from Pennsylvania's sweltering humid summers was to swim in the Monongahela River, carefully avoiding coal barges and locks with dangerous currents.

You walked to and from school in sub-zero temperatures without boots or water-repellent clothing. Your simple walking shoes with flat heels were good enough and you were lucky to get a hand-me-down jacket from one of your brothers.

You hauled coal from the cellar and took a turn shoveling it into the furnace in winter and washed clothes in a roller-pin washer and hung clothes to dry on a clothesline stretched across your mother's backyard garden. You dutifully tended the garden with your mother and rested on a back porch glider, a teenager sitting like an old woman contemplating her exit.

Under different circumstances, you would have gone to college, but that wasn't economically feasible for your family or culturally promoted for a woman in a poor blue-collar mining and factory town in the 1930s. Instead, you went to work as an underage waitress in a local dancehall and then as a clerk in a five-and-dime store. Welcome to your life.

Your sister went to work in the same glassware factory where your father worked and two of your brothers also went to work in factories. Your third brother went first to the Navy and then became a merchant seaman.

You married a military man and lived where his assignments sent him, including Germany and several US states. You endured long periods of an absent husband due to WWII, the Korean Conflict, and the Vietnam War.

Without a driver's license, you toted groceries on the city bus and took taxis to doctor's appointments.

You learned the hard way that the US soldier you married demanded strict enforcement of chain-of-command orders in his household but had trouble obeying them with his superior officers in uniform. You saved his career on multiple occasions by intervening on his behalf when he had acted impulsively and disobeyed orders with self-righteous indignation.

Throughout nearly seventy years of married life, you sheltered in place and created a domestic world caring for your family.

How I wish I could have been there when you were a young girl needing glasses to see the blackboard in school. How I wish I could have put a bicycle under a Christmas tree and taught you to ride it on the sooty streets and uneven sidewalks of your hometown of Charleroi, Pennsylvania. How I wish I could have taught you to drive when you were a teenager and bought you a car to expand your horizon. How I wish I could have encouraged you to go to college and paid for your tuition. How I wish I would have insisted more forcefully that you learn to write checks and pay bills before your eighth decade of life and your husband needed your help in these mundane but essential matters. How I wish I could have more successfully convinced your husband that your opinion counted and shouldn't be discounted due to your gender. How I wish I could have helped you enjoy more independence and freedom in your life.

You lived where my father wanted to live, under his conditions, habits, rules, and temperament. You were his dutiful servant for nearly seventy years, cooking all his meals, doing all his laundry, cleaning all his spilled coffee and breadcrumbs, listening to all his life's grievances and disappointments. How I wish I could have convinced him to listen with a more attentive and empathetic ear to your grievances and disappointments, which more than matched his.

I hope that before you left this world I was able to acknowledge your strengths of character and intellect. You lived a morally righteous life in faithful service to your husband, daughter, and me. I hope that I was able to convey how awed I was by your ability to complete the *Los Angeles Times* Sunday crossword puzzle in ink every week with religious fervor, or how inspired I was by your ability to read three books per week until the age of ninety even when your eyes could only endure one, or how impressed I was when you would outmaneuver your husband and peers in games of bridge, or how happy I was to see you delighted to whip up gourmet meals to tickle the taste buds of family and friends. Under different circumstances and in another time, you surely would have become a member of the professional class and impacted the world on a much wider scale.

Thank you for never becoming the bitter person you had every right to become. Thank you for the warm, loving home you provided me. Thank you for the life you gave me that you were not able to give yourself.

DEAR FATHER,

You pushed a wheelbarrow in a steel mill for five years, starting when you were only sixteen. You worked a graveyard shift and went directly from the job to your high school classes for your junior and senior years. You tried to stay awake and learn something; your teachers forgave you when you fell asleep, knowing you were helping your family pay bills and buy food. Five brothers and two sisters demand a lot of upkeep. You were promoted through to graduation with courtesy Ds. Somehow you became exceptionally literate. You taught me to read and understand newspaper articles when I was five and I sought out your expertise as an expert grammarian all of my adult life, most conspicuously during my college years earning a degree in English.

You erased your lifelong burden of shame at not possessing a college degree by taking classes at our local community college and then transferring to a four-year institution when you were in your mid-fifties, still working full time. You surprised everyone by choosing a course in human sexuality as you worked to fulfill your general education requirements. After watching a film in class showing a couple having sex, you made only one comment: "How could people with such filthy feet have sex?" I recall that my mother asked you, "So, you spent the whole time looking at the soles of the couple's feet?" I said nothing, fidgeted in my seat, and prayed for divine intervention to relieve me of my discomfort. But the conversation made sense to me. In your mind, if a small part of something was amiss, then the whole thing was spoiled. Your perspective functioned as a motivating force for achievement and a hindrance to contentment all your life.

We each earned a college degree in the same year, 1977. I was prouder of your accomplishment than mine. You ordered a class ring, and I did not. On occasions when you wore it, the ring opened the door to many wonderful recollections of how you attended evening classes on your way home from work and studied late into the evening and in the wee hours of the morning before your commute and workday began. You were a rugged and resolute fifty-eight years young when your degree was bestowed.

In your lifetime of military service, you rose from enlisted man to lieutenant colonel while completing tours of duty in WWII, Korea, and Vietnam (twice). When pressed to speak about your experiences of war, you were always reluctant to respond. The most one could get out of you was, "It was a job, and I did what needed to be done."

Whenever we were out together and you saw a young person in uniform, you excused yourself and went over to him or her and engaged in a whispered conversation. Then you slipped the individual folded-up currency under a breakfast plate or into a pocket. Your act was never one of condescension. It was your way of thanking the person for choosing a difficult path in life that you were intimately familiar with.

After retiring from the US Army, you worked as a Veterans

Benefits Administration counselor, evaluating (and when appropriate advocating for) disability claims on behalf of soldiers who had served and suffered in Vietnam. You helped countless veterans who were dealing with physical, mental, and emotional conditions get the help they deserved from the government in the form of treatment and disability payments.

After you retired from the VA, you continued assisting veterans on a pro bono basis by giving them wise counsel, reopening their disability claims that had initially been denied, writing letters of appeal, filling out requisite paperwork, and helping them navigate the bureaucratic maze of government. You continued this informal work until your late eighties. Once again, this was your way of saying thank you to people who had chosen a difficult path in life and had paid a high price for their choice.

In your final years, you needed a walker to get around, but you used it rarely. You cursed it continuously, calling it "a goddamned wheelbarrow." I would say, "Dad, you're not in the steel mill anymore. It's just a device to help you keep your balance." You were unconvinced. "It's a goddamned wheelbarrow. Take it away." You knew that the walker was not a wheelbarrow. Calling it that was just your way of showing your contempt for it and letting go of the anger you felt as you contended with your body's limitations.

I lost you in 2010. I feel your loss every day. You were my greatest teacher, my greatest role model, my greatest example of what it means to push with all one's might to fulfill one's duty. I've never seen anyone push harder.

I cannot thank you enough for everything you were in life and everything you still are in death.

CHAPTER 44:
Moving On

DEAR MOTHER,

By teaching me how to die, you have taught me how to live. All through your life, you were a paragon of stoicism and resilience. You rarely called attention to yourself; you rarely expressed notions of self-pity or disappointment at how things didn't work out the way you would have liked. You accepted disappointment in a matter-of-fact manner. You took deep breaths and moved on.

As you neared the end of your life, you called me on the phone and told me that I better get myself down to see you. You didn't explicitly say that your time was near, but I knew that was what you meant.

You were in a rehabilitation center for the third time in as many years. You were blessed with astonishingly good health until you reached your early nineties. Even then, you had no history of surgeries or a complicated regimen of medications to take. You took a blood pressure pill, mostly as a precaution. Doctor's visits were short and uneventful, beyond the doctor remarking on your thin, relatively clean medical history chart.

Then, very late in life, you suffered a few falls, resulting in fractures, necessitating stays in rehab facilities. The pattern of falls and fractures exasperated your patience, and I know the stays in rehab were barely endurable for you. The settings were always stale and drab, permeated by the sickening smells of ammonia and rubbing alcohol. The routine of nurses checking your vital signs every two hours was maddening. The therapy sessions were painful and exhausting. Yet, you persevered, complaining only of loud TVs and roommates who never seemed to sleep.

When I arrived at the rehab center, I found you in a mental state I had never seen before. You were engaged in a conversation with invisible and enigmatic forces—memories, demons, God?? The conversation didn't really involve me, but you wanted me to witness it. I ineffectively tried to console you, but you were beyond consolation. Upon reflection, I think you were conversing with death itself. I'm really not sure if you were embroiled in argument or agreement.

A few days later, you lost the ability to form comprehensible words. But you continued speaking. You became more accepting of the rehab center, of your wheelchair, of the loud TV, and of your insomnious roommate. You delighted in going out to a small garden area, where you looked at everything with eyes wide and appreciative—the blue sky, the clouds, the flower beds, the other patients, the hustling nurses, and the worried visitors. You talked constantly, seeming to give your good wishes to everything and everyone.

On your final day on earth, a nurse told us that she went into your room, checked on you, determined that you were doing just fine, and left. A few minutes later, she entered your room again to discover that you had expired. You left this world in the same manner that you lived your life—quietly, unassumingly, stoically, unobtrusively, without complaint. I regret not being with you at the end. I imagine that you took a deep breath and moved on.

If I could only have another moment to tell you how much I admire you, how much I'm in awe of your strength and resilience, and how much I learned from you, I would take it in a flash; I fear that I did not convey those sentiments emphatically enough while you were here. I pray that in another realm I have a chance to make up for this failure.

PART NINE: IN MEMORIAM

DEAR DARLENE,

I suppose this is a kind of progress report to you, my beloved wife. I recently marked the sixth anniversary of your death from breast cancer. To everyone who says that time heals all wounds, or the sense of loss eventually subsides and becomes easier to accept, I'm living proof that those sentiments are wrong.

I'll admit that the shock of your passing—at the tender age of fifty, after a seven-year fight—has lost some intensity. But when I allow myself to relive each moment of your final days, and the long string of moments stretching back to the diagnosis of your disease, the intensity returns in full force, and I'm left devastated and incapacitated. Conscious effort is required to keep the memories from metastasizing and crushing all over again my spirit and soul.

I try to keep up the necessary effort, but sometimes I give in and relive everything in excruciating detail. I feel I owe that to you. It is my way of saying thank you for our time together and for allowing me to bear witness to the relentless battle you waged and the manner in which you faced every vile trait of dying with such fearless resolve.

Most days, I pray that you are with God and reunited with all of your deceased loved ones, enjoying an afterlife that is free of all the pain and loss you endured with so much courage and grace here on Earth. I look up at the sky, most often at night, and ask God to take care of you. I pray that you are in another realm, doing there what you could no longer do here.

These days, I'm mostly sad that you have not been here to see how our sons have matured. Trent was a tender sixteen years old when he had to say goodbye to you. His graduation from high school was a golden culmination of all the personal and academic grit and integrity he displayed from his earliest days. He told me after the ceremony that he felt your presence as he sat on the field where we watched him play soccer, listening for his name to be called, and receiving his diploma. He wears your presence around his neck every day, along with the silver medallion you gave him when he started high school.

Now he is finishing his last year of college, majoring in actuarial math. I know that would make you happy, as math was your favorite subject. He is closing the ends of a circle in a way that would surely make your heart leap with joyful pride.

Trent is loving, sensitive, and oh-so-smart. His love has sustained me through some of my darkest moments.

By the way, he is a rugged six feet, four inches tall. For me, hugging him is like climbing a tree.

When John-Michael lost you, he was just shy of his twenty-fifth birthday. It's hard to fathom that he will soon be turning thirty-one. He stands six feet and two inches. When Trent and John-Michael walk side by side, I feel as though I'm swimming in their shadows.

Because he was not living at home during your illness, as Trent was, I think your death initially hit John-Michael harder than it hit Trent.

I'm thrilled to tell you that John-Michael earned his art degree at California State University, Northridge, in 2018. He proved himself to be quite a capable student, spending several semesters on the Dean's List.

His graduation was quite spectacular. The setting on the university campus was beautifully decorated and lit, giving the ceremony a storybook quality. The graduates sat in a lush bowl, encircled by lovely trees and shrubbery. I felt transposed to a different reality. I'm hoping that John-Michael felt something similar.

In the photos we took afterwards, John-Michael looked happier than I have ever seen him look. His smile was radiant, and it stayed on his face for a long time afterwards. It was a sight that I think would have made you feel as though God was caressing your heart.

You will not be surprised to know that John-Michael has evolved into a skilled photographer, a serious student of music, a talented writer, a self-taught guitarist, and an amateur tattoo artist.

When I'm with him, I know that he carries you in his delicate yet rugged soul.

I asked him to design a tattoo to honor you, and he created a beautiful image of the Christian cross and breast cancer ribbon intertwined. We sat at our dining room table one night and he tattooed his design on my forearm. I wear it proudly and I'm so enamored with his creation and grateful to him for making it a permanent part of my body.

I'm hesitant to tell you that John-Michael has spent some time working in San Francisco as an Uber/Lyft driver. I know you would have feared him entrusting his safety to strangers in a big city at all hours of the night. You would no doubt have worried yourself to exhaustion. I'm happy to say that he survived that experience, his customers treated him well, and he has some stories to tell that I hope one day he conveys in a book.

I'm overjoyed to tell you that he has been in Japan for the last year, teaching English. I'm extremely proud of him, and I know you and I would have traveled to see him at least once by now. He started out working at a rural school on a lesser island, but recently he was able to transfer to a school in Tokyo. I'm so happy about that, knowing that he will be able to connect with a much larger group of native English speakers. I expect he will stay for another year at least. The fact that I taught English in Japan some four decades ago gives our experiences a satisfying symmetry.

John-Michael and I have had some wonderful conversations in the last few years and I'm excited to see what decisions he makes in the future.

Both of our boys have developed into young men that you would be so proud of. You wisely and courageously prepared them to go through this world without a mother physically present. They have each honored you by pursuing their interests and dreams, and they have not used your death as an excuse to give up on their own lives or to lose themselves in self-pity, anger, or bitterness.

I pray that you are able to keep watch over their lives. They will always need you. They carry you in their hearts. They feel your presence. I will always need you. I carry you in my heart. I feel your presence. My prayers give me solace. I thank you every day for all of it.